Cavalry Hero
Casimir Pulaski

Portraits in Faith and Freedom

SET 2: POLISH ADVOCATES OF HOPE
AND NATIONHOOD

So Young a Queen: Jadwiga of Poland
by Dorothy Adams

Cavalry Hero: Casimir Pulaski
by Ruth and Paul Hume

The Lion of Poland: The Story of Paderewski
by Lois Mills

Cavalry Hero
Casimir Pulaski

by Dorothy Adams

Illustrated by Irena Lorentowicz

BETHLEHEM BOOKS • IGNATIUS PRESS
Bathgate   San Francisco

Print book originally published by
P.J. Kenedy & Sons, New York, 1957

Cover art by Roseanne Sharpe
Illustrations by Irena Lorentowicz
Maps and added material © 2016 Bethlehem Books
Mapwork by Margaret Rasmussen
Cover design by Melissa Sobotta

Revised edition
All Rights Reserved

First Bethlehem Books Printing May 2018

ISBN 978-1-932350-74-6
Library of Congress Control Number 2017956055

Bethlehem Books • Ignatius Press
10194 Garfield Street South
Bathgate, ND 58216
www.bethlehembooks.com

Printed in the United States on acid-free paper

Manufactured by Thomson-Shore, Dexter, MI (USA); RMA233JM42, June, 2018

Statement on Portraits in Faith and Freedom

Bethlehem Books is bringing back this series of biographies originally made available in the 1950s and 60s by publishers who wished to introduce young people to a wide range of arresting and faithful Catholic lives. Slightly edited now for the modern reader, these biographies present key people and events from the past that help us reflect anew on the meaning of freedom. They depict how powerfully men and women of faith can form and influence the world in which they live.

About Usage of Outdated Terms

In republishing the books that form our *Portraits in Faith and Freedom* series, the editors considered whether it would be worthwhile to update the authors' usage of words like "Indian" and "Negro." The more current preference among many is "Native American" and "African American." The editors found, however, that changing the original terms often did not work well for the context of those times. The attitudes of respect and honesty that inspired these works—written in the 1950s and early 1960s—clearly conveyed the authors' positive meaning. In most cases, therefore, we have let the words stand.

Bethlehem Books

TO MAJA, EVA,
ANNJA AND ANDREW

Contents

Maps
Pronunciation Guide

1.	*At Winiary*	1
2.	*Boyhood*	17
3.	*The Knights*	32
4.	*The Polish Confederates*	51
5.	*Exile and Prison*	71
6.	*The American Dream*	80
7.	*Washington's Aide*	92
8.	*Winter of Disappointment*	111
9.	*Pulaski's Legion*	124
10.	*Treachery at Little Egg Harbor*	137
11.	*Victory at Charleston*	151
12.	*The Battle of Savannah*	168
13.	*A Hero's End*	188

About the Author	197
Historical Insights by Daria Sockey	199

Timeline
List of Titles in Portraits in Faith and Freedom

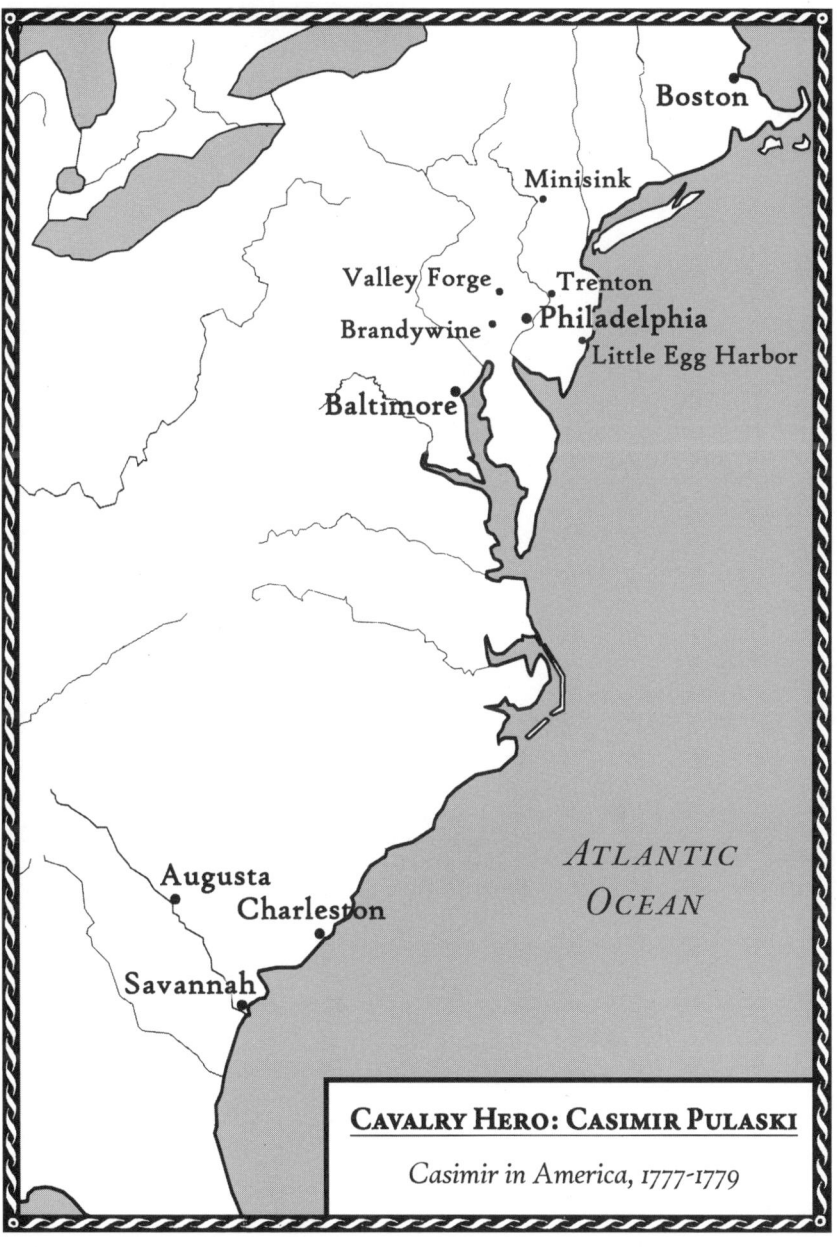

Pronunciation Guide

How to Pronounce a Few Polish Places and Names

PLACES
  Winiary = VIN ya ry
  Cracow = CRAC ow
  Czestochowa = Ches tuh HOH vah
  Lwow = leVOHF

RIVER
  Dnieper = NEE pr (rhymes with "keeper")

NAME
  Poniatowski = Pon ya TOF ski

1

At Winiary

AT THE TIME of Casimir Pulaski's birth, Poland was at peace. He was born on March 4, 1747, the second son of Joseph Pulaski, a rich and very successful lawyer. This law practice had brought Count Pulaski an enormous fortune. Instead of money, he had preferred being paid in land, and during his lifetime he had become one of the greatest landowners in Poland.

He lived in a rambling, white-columned homestead called Winiary where he had taken his bride after their marriage and where all his eight children were born. It was situated in Podolia, a province of southeast Poland which was near the perilous Russian border.

The news of Casimir's birth spread in that swift way news traveled by word of mouth in a time when there was neither telephone nor telegraph. At once all the friends and relatives of the Pulaski family packed into their lumbering horse-drawn coaches or jumped into their saddles to set off for Winiary.

In those days baptisms were the occasions for great celebrations. They were considered as a wonderful opportunity for getting together and seeing friends and acquaintances from all parts of Poland. The journey was an added excuse to visit still others as stops for the night were made on the way. The baptism of Casimir provided countless people with the pretext for a trip and a holiday.

Winiary was in a commotion of preparation for the great number of guests certain to arrive. Meats were turning on the roasting spits over the fire in the kitchen. The guest wings opening out on the gardens were being cleared and aired. Huntsmen were searching the woods for game: deer, pheasant and wild boar, while fishermen combed the streams and lakes for pike and carp. Smoke curled above the bakehouses where piles of bread were raked from the coals. The pantry maids fashioned cakes and pastries and the steward decanted wine from the oak casks in the cellar.

But the greatest excitement was in the dining room where the feast was being laid out on the table, extended to its full length, and the sideboards were already groaning with china and glass. Everything was being put in readiness for a two weeks' celebration. Some guests might stay but a day or two, some would remain a week, but others would surely come to take their place. All in all, several hundred visitors were expected.

The old housekeeper oversaw all the preparations. She was determined to keep her mistress, Countess Pulaska, the baby's mother, in bed and away from the excitement. She bustled about the bedroom, her black taffeta petticoat rustling as she laid out the robe in which, two years before, Francis, Casimir's older brother, was baptized and his father and grandfather before him. The lace-ruffled and embroidered pillow on which the child would be held was properly pressed and trimmed with new ribbons.

The two older sisters, Anna and Josepha, would not play in their room, but stayed sitting on their mother's bed begging to see their new brother.

"You spoil them, Madame. You should rest," the housekeeper scolded in vain, as the nurse in her gay linen dress, embroidered with red poppies and blue cornflowers, laid the baby in Countess Pulaska's arms.

Then the aunt who was to be Casimir's godmother appeared in the doorway. "Everyone is in the chapel," she announced, and added with a smile, "Hurry; all is ready and waiting."

While the housekeeper hastened to tie Casimir on his gorgeous ruffled pillow and arrange the huge bow, his sisters jumped and skipped about him in great excitement. It seemed as though the housekeeper would never be satisfied with the appearance of her charge, but at last she placed him in his godmother's arms. The procession swept out of the room, the nurse steadying the pillow and the old housekeeper leading the little girls firmly by their hands.

The chapel, built at the rear of the house at the end of the entrance hall, was reached through Joseph Pulaski's study. It was decorated in gold and white, the ceiling painted blue like the sky with angels peeping out between floating clouds. As it was not large enough to hold all the guests, most of the men were standing either in the hall or in the study, where they could exchange bits of news and watch the ceremony through the open doors. As Casimir was borne in on his godmother's arms, they stopped chatting with Father Mark, the kindly, black-bearded Carmelite priest who lived with the family. In silence Casimir was brought to the font, and Father Mark began intoning the prayers. When the baby wailed lustily in protest as the water trickled over his head, everyone agreed that this was a good sign. It was an old Polish saying that if the child cried loudly he was putting up strong resistance to the devil.

Casimir's earliest recollection was of his father, holding him in a saddle, and leading the horse down the sandy driveway to the village gate. He never forgot the warmth of the strong, affectionate embrace that steadied him, or the smell of the sweet-scented lime trees, the home of countless families of birds chirping and singing high in the branches over his head. On their return his mother, who was standing in the shadow of the pillared portico, had waved and called "Bravo."

When Casimir was five his brother Anthony was born. By that time two more sisters had come into the world, but their births had occurred quietly, almost unnoticed. The day Anthony was born, however, his father promised Casimir the pony that had hitherto belonged to his older brother Francis. Francis, his father said, was now big enough to have the young Arabian mare.

As soon as the commotion over Anthony's baptism had subsided and the guests had all gone home, Count Pulaski called to Casimir to go with him to the stable. "I want you to learn how to handle a horse properly," he explained, as the two walked hand in hand.

"But I know how to ride," Casimir boasted.

His father smiled. He had watched his son bouncing along the driveway, the pony sauntering or jogging as he pleased.

In the stables they found old Michael the coachman who was ordering the grooms about with a lordly air. Tactfully Joseph Pulaski waited to speak until Michael noticed them.

"I'm putting Casimir in your hands," he then said. "He is to stay in the paddock until you feel satisfied he has full control of his mount. While I am far away in Warsaw you are in charge, and you decide when to let him go out with Francis."

So for the next few months Casimir rode round and round the paddock beside a groom under the exacting eye of Michael. The coachman never praised the boy however carefully he went through his paces. At a certain place he had to canter, at another gallop, then bring his pony to a trot in a split second. Old Michael accepted no excuses. "Either you know how to ride a horse or you don't," he would say sternly. "You don't leave the paddock for the fields until you do!"

There was no use in asking his mother to come to watch him ride in order to persuade Michael to let him go out sooner with Francis. Everything around the stables and the horses was under the old coachman's rule. Nor would he have hesitated to tell Countess Pulaska, "The boy doesn't go out until *I* say he is ready to."

Although Casimir had early proved he was fearless, he now tried to learn how to be patient, for

he was naturally impetuous and quick of temper. Michael would not be hurried, and he taught Casimir to ride with great precision.

"You need your right hand free for your gun when you go hunting," Michael explained. "You must hold the bridle only with your left. In an emergency, when both hands are needed, you will have to guide the horse with your knees." Casimir was then shown how to jump over logs, and finally over a path the width of a stream which wound through the meadows.

At the end of the summer, he made his first trip to the woods with the groom and Francis. Old Michael drove down the lane to watch them clear the brook. The wind whistled in Casimir's ears as he flew across rolling farm land, stretching as far as he could see, the grain sparkling and dancing in the sun. Rabbits kicked up their white tails and scuttled into hiding. The larks circled overhead, and from far off he heard the peasants singing in rhythm with their work. He never forgot the joy of that first wild, free ride.

That evening when he boasted to his mother that he could jump as well as Francis, she remarked, "Don't forget, dear, pride comes before a fall. Watch carefully that tomorrow you do as well as today." Marianne Pulaska adored her children but she never spoiled them.

However, Casimir's older sisters, who could ride as well as he, hugged him. They loved their dauntless little five-year-old brother with his curling yellow hair, intelligent eyes and sturdy figure. Anna was especially devoted. She was happy he could now take her place riding with Francis. At eleven she felt quite grown up and preferred to accompany her mother on the morning round of visits in the village. She was already talking about becoming a nun.

The younger sister, Josepha, however, was always undecided whether to join her mother or her brothers. She loved to play tag on horseback, too, and when neighboring children drove over to Winiary with their parents for tea, it was she who led the way to the stables and organized the game.

Francis was already a fine horseman. He could ride as fast and wheel as abruptly as much older boys. But he often stole back to the house to listen quietly to the conversation about the tea table. Everyone predicted he would be a lawyer and a statesman like his father when he grew up.

When he was six Casimir was sent to the nearby parish school which Francis, Anna and Josepha also attended. He had already learned to read and write at home, and now he began to study Latin. The lessons were not too difficult, and in the afternoon he and his friends played at stalking Cossacks in the forest. Behind each tree lurked an enemy. The boys used wooden lances which they made themselves, and as they dashed about the forest they would hack down the sapling trees which represented their foe.

As they grew older they learned to shoot so straight that they could hit a bull's-eye at full gallop. They loved to set up apples on the fence posts and to split them apart. When the wind was blowing, they tied a light board to a branch to make a moving target and would shoot at it as they cantered past. These games were to prove very useful when they grew older and play turned into the sad reality of war.

During Casimir's childhood, however, no one thought of war or invasions. Podolia was so peaceful that no one locked his doors at night. The roads were guarded by little shrines to Our Lady at Częstochowa to whom everyone, peasant and noble alike, made a pilgrimage at one time or another in their lives.

It was the children's privilege to serve these pilgrims and all the beggars who stopped at Winiary. They had been taught the old Polish saying, "The guest in the home is Christ in the home." Casimir's five sisters were generally first to spy the beggar trudging up the driveway and first into the kitchen to fetch the bowl of soup and loaf of bread always at hand.

Very early one morning, a few days after his eighth birthday, Casimir went out to visit his new Arabian horse before anyone else was stirring. A light snow crunched crisply under his boots as he skipped down the four stone steps of the portico to the drive and hurried around the corner of the house. He was just thinking what name he would give his horse when he noticed a figure hunched against the cookhouse door. The cook was starting breakfast, but as the door was closed he had probably not heard the stranger's knock.

In place of "Good morning," Casimir politely said, "Let Jesus Christ be praised."

"For endless ages, amen," replied an old man who looked up into his eyes with a piercing sadness. Casimir felt in his pocket. There was a little silver coin and a gold piece he had received on his birthday. He pulled out the gold piece and handed it to the old man. Ashamed to have the beggar thank him, he began banging on the door with all his strength, for the lock was too stiff for him to turn. When the cook opened the door, Casimir said, "Quick, quick, there is an old man fallen in the snow."

He turned to point out the beggar, but the old man was gone. They ran to the driveway but there was no one in sight. The place where the beggar had stood was clearly marked in the snow—but there were no footprints anywhere. So they circled back to the kitchen, the cook shaking his head and making the sign of the cross.

"Truly," he said, "that was truly Jesus Christ himself!" He gently drew Casimir into the kitchen and closed the door. "Come, sit by the fire to warm yourself, and I will give you some milk."

As long as he lived Casimir would never forget the searching eyes of the old beggar. He felt the single coin in his pocket. The gold piece was gone. It was not a dream.

"My mother," the cook told him, "had such an experience long ago. She found an old man near the crossroad crucifix to whom she gave the bread and milk she was carrying to my father who was plowing. This man told her the Cossacks were coming to raid the village. She should warn my father and hide as fast as possible. Then the old man disappeared without leaving a trace. When my mother got over her surprise, she snatched up my brother and me and rushed out to the fields, for she already heard the thunder of the Cossack horses' hoofs. She called my father, and we hid under some bushes in a sort of ravine at the side of the meadow.

"The Cossacks caught the other farmers who were plowing and slashed off their heads. They carried away all the young women and children in the village and killed the men. Then they set fire to the place. Today, when I shut my eyes, I still hear the shouting and screaming; the crackle of the fire burning our log cabins and the roar of the thatched roofs. The fires in the village blazed all night. Next morning my father saw the Cossacks had gone. They had taken our cows. There was nothing left but ashes where our house and barn had stood and no living creature in the whole village. We were very hungry. My father and mother carried us to another place. That is why we came to Masovia. Father never wanted to go back."

Casimir was much impressed by this story. He had heard many times about the Cossacks. He had played at fighting them every day in the forest with the other children, but they seemed more legendary than real. "Do they still make raids?" he asked. "Can't the Polish soldiers stop them?"

"It's a mighty big country for our soldiers to defend," the cook explained. "I don't know how many months it takes to travel from one end of the frontier to the other. It goes all the way from the Baltic to the Black Sea." Though Casimir nodded wisely he had no idea where those oceans lay.

Casimir believed he should ask his father about the Cossacks. Although he had always felt very close to his mother, he was afraid of worrying her. Of course he repeated the story the cook had told him to Francis, and the boys decided they should wait until their father came home for Easter.

As the time for Count Pulaski's arrival drew near, every afternoon instead of playing in the woods Casimir and Francis rode through the village of Winiary and out on the Warsaw highway, hoping to meet their father's coach. They were rewarded after a few days by seeing the familiar horses pulling the heavy traveling coach into the turn on the deep-cut road into the Winiary Valley. They shot off at a gallop and soon had drawn alongside. The second coachman was struggling with the horses who were trotting briskly on the last lap of the long journey. Count Pulaski leaned out of the window and called to them with pride in his voice. While a groom held the horses, the boys climbed into the coach to embrace their father. Then, mounting one of the boys' horses and leading the other, the groom followed the coach the rest of the way home.

Casimir's patience had been strained to the breaking point. He burst out with the cook's story and asked his father to explain why the Polish Army could not protect the eastern provinces of their country from such dreadful things.

"Dearest son," Joseph sadly replied, "no one wants to listen when I talk about needing a strong army. They won't vote the taxes for it. Everyone seems deluded by the idea that Poland is so strong it doesn't need armies any more."

"Poland is the biggest country in all Europe," Francis added proudly. "Who would be afraid of Bavaria, Hanover, Saxony, Austria, or Prussia or any of the hundred other little German states!"

"But the Cossacks," Casimir interrupted. "If they are just wild bands, as Francis says, how can they raid Poland?"

"It's because they hide in the whole vast empty steppes, and it is easy for them to make surprise attacks and then disappear before our people can get help. Besides, the Russians encourage them to come our way just so they will leave Moscow and St. Petersburg in peace," Joseph explained.

"Can't you do something?" Casimir asked.

"I can talk, and I do, but everyone laughs at me," Joseph replied.

He was still frowning a little and shaking his head when they came to the door of Winiary, for Casimir's question was exactly what he himself was worrying about just then.

2

Boyhood

NO ONE was ever more happy to be at home with his family than Joseph Pulaski, for he had to be away much of the time. When he was not in Warsaw, the Polish capital, or attending the Diets, which were the assemblies governing the country, or engaged in legal battles for his clients, he was occupied in the business of running the one hundred and eight farms and villages and the fourteen towns which he had acquired in payment of his legal fees. These farms and towns were scattered throughout Poland and he often traveled from one of them to the other.

While on the road, however, he would prepare his next speeches for the Diets where he was known for his eloquence and his presence was always an event. The Polish Diets were very powerful. They elected the King, voted taxes and decided all questions of state. Their weakness lay in the right of any one of its members to stand up and say, "I veto." Then that Diet was dissolved. Fortunately this right was rarely used, but the very threat of it inclined everyone to compromise. Joseph Pulaski was one of the leaders who constantly pointed out the weakness of this system. He also pleaded for a reorganized modern standing army.

It was true that King Augustus III had a personal guard, as did all the great Polish nobles, and although there was a small Polish army, it was poorly armed and inadequate for the protection of such an immense country. The great lords who were depended upon to supply militia for defense had allowed their private armies to degenerate into guards of honor gorgeously attired in fancy uniforms and with little real experience in warfare.

Joseph Pulaski met with disagreement when he urged the Diets to increase the national army. For one thing it seemed to most people like giving more power to the King, and they had no desire to do this because they considered King Augustus just a figurehead. Besides, he was bound by ties of blood to other reigning monarchs in Europe and they did not entirely trust him.

So at the meetings of the Diets all the applause went to those who talked about the brotherhood of nations or who boasted Poland had proved itself the most mighty state in Europe. Within the memory of some still living, German ambassadors had fallen on their knees before an earlier Polish king, pleading with him to protect Europe from the Turks. After the Polish armies defeated the Turks at Vienna in 1683, the last threat to the peace of Europe seemed to have been removed.

People were tired of war and wartime taxation. They were intent on building up new industries and trade in a peaceful world. Whenever Joseph Pulaski stood up to speak in a Diet about measures for defense he was shouted down. "If you build up the army," he was told, "you will frighten our neighbors into doing the same. Armies breed wars. Soldiers have nothing else to do but fight." This sounded logical to almost everyone.

"We have no army, yet look at the one the Russians are building!" Count Pulaski retorted.

"The Russians have enough lawless Tartars and Cossacks and boyars to keep five armies busy," someone laughed.

This particular Easter Joseph Pulaski was indeed glad to be home again, and far away from Warsaw and all those vexing problems. But he was the magistrate of Wareck, the neighboring city, and spokesman for the district, so while he was in Winiary there were always twenty or thirty guests for dinner, men who came to consult him on civil and political affairs. No one in the neighborhood hesitated to arrive in the morning and remain until late afternoon. They were certain of a warm and cordial welcome.

Casimir was now allowed to sit down to dinner with the guests, a privilege Francis and his older sisters already enjoyed. His father felt that this younger son had earned his place by the questions he had asked about his country's safety. During the next four years he was often to listen intently to the men's discussion of national affairs and to hear the heated arguments of both sides.

Happy as he was to welcome his neighbors to his home, Joseph looked forward each day to a quiet evening with his wife, his children and Father Mark. In the afternoon the priest always joined the family for coffee to hear the latest news and then would read vespers in the chapel where everyone, including the servants, knelt together.

After supper Countess Pulaska would play on the spinet and sing with a bird-clear voice the fashionable French and Italian songs of the period, her fine features silhouetted against the candlelight. She was slightly built, and in spite of the care of eight children she seemed very young. She had dark hair piled high on her head and curling about her ears. When she spoke, she enchanted everyone with her direct dark eyes and her habit of giving each person her closest attention. She had a bewitching smile that captivated not only her husband and her children but guests and servants as well.

Although she seemed so gentle, she had an iron will. She never faltered or hesitated in making decisions, but they were well thought out and so reasonable that it was logical to follow them. While her husband was away, she planned where crops were to be planted in each field; she kept the buildings in repair and checked over all the accounts. She settled the knotty problems of the peasants in the village so deftly that they seemed to evaporate as she spoke, and she really practiced her deeply pious belief in Christian love.

If Marianne was the practical member of the family, Joseph was the idealist. Unlike those politicians who are always looking for momentary compromise, Joseph saw black as black, and white as white. His famous eloquence was due to his unshaken belief in absolute justice.

He was a man of middle height, firmly built, with sandy hair which in his youth had been blond. He was cheerful and affectionate and loved his family with an unusually tender understanding. Although he was a scholar and knew the Latin classics so well they were part of his usual speech, he was no pedant. He belonged to the world in which he lived, and used its brilliant epigrams, only with him they did not sound hollow. He never accepted work unless he was entirely satisfied his client's claims were just. When he took a law case, he did not leave it until he had won every single point.

At twelve, after six years in the parish school, Casimir had to leave his beloved family and go to a high school in Warsaw where his father owned another house since he spent so much time there. Casimir studied with the Theatine Fathers. There was a more modern school in Warsaw, but Count Pulaski chose for his son the old-fashioned classical curriculum of the Theatines—Latin classics, composition, literature, some arithmetic, but no sciences.

It was the education then considered best fitted for a landowner and statesman.

By day Joseph worked on his law practice and Casimir attended school. But in the evening Count Pulaski introduced his son to the sights and social life of the capital, including the receptions of the King.

King Augustus was a patron of the arts—sculpture, poetry, architecture, music and painting. He decorated his lovely palace overhanging the Vistula River with a fine collection of Italian masters. Every evening he held court with a concert which was open to everyone in Warsaw society. After the concert, the dining room doors opened on a table, seventy feet long, piled high with every delicacy of the culinary art. Crystal candelabra, reflected in gilt-framed mirrors lining the walls, blazed with the light of myriads of dancing flames. Casimir, who had never seen so much light at night, or heard such roars of laughter or clashing of silver against china, was too stunned to speak.

His father thought it was very important for Casimir to learn court etiquette, courtly manners and courtly conversation. A gentleman was judged by the way he entered a room, bowed, and by the ease and grace with which he turned a compliment. Casimir was not a country bumpkin, and Joseph wished to see him at ease wherever he went. He also wished him to have some training in the use of arms.

So when the boy was fifteen, to finish his education his father sent him to the court of the Duke of Courland, then a fiefdom of the Polish Crown. Today called Latvia, Courland was situated north of Lithuania near the Baltic Sea on the Russian frontier. It was at least a four weeks' journey from Winiary.

The young Duke of Courland held political ideas similar to those of Count Pulaski. In fact, he was being groomed as the future king by those in opposition to the policies of the present one. Hence he was surrounded by those who wanted a strong army and were afraid of the growing Russian power.

For his new life as a page at the Court of Courland, Casimir was outfitted with embroidered waistcoats, lace-ruffled linen shirts, satin knee breeches and flowered damask coats. For his journey he was provided with a broadcloth suit trimmed with gold braid, covered by a wide cape to protect him from rain or cold. Dressed in the family livery, one of the grooms with whom he had grown up was to accompany him.

On the morning he was to leave, all his belongings, packed in wooden cases, were strapped to a light surrey, an extra horse tied behind. The groom brought the two saddle horses up to the portico where all the family and Father Mark had assembled to bid him good-bye. It was the first time Casimir had left both his parents to go so far away, but he was too much excited by the bustle of preparation to be sad.

On his long journey to Courland he spent some nights with old family friends, others at houses where he had letters of introduction, and still others at lodgings which he had to arrange on the way. At each house he was given directions to the next. He passed through the lake country and great primeval forests that stretch north and east into Russia, and where he had to be on the alert against the attack of wolves, bear and wild boar. He stopped in Vilno, the ancient capital of Lithuania, and arrived at his destination after five weeks of travel.

The Duke and Duchess of Courland welcomed their new page warmly. The Duchess, Francesca Krasinska, was very beautiful and only eighteen years old. She had known the Pulaski family since childhood and was as tactful as she was level-headed. Casimir immediately became her willing slave and tried to follow her every suggestion. In her company he learned all the intricacies of court manners, and soon became at ease in his surroundings. The Duchess found Casimir's enthusiasm and loyalty delightful, and her friendship and balanced judgment became truly invaluable to him.

Above all, Casimir had been sent to Courland so that he might learn the military arts. He drilled with the Duke's soldiers and spent every morning practicing the intricate use of a lance which required not only great power in the wrist but skill as well. He was already a fine shot, but he learned still more feats with the pistol. To build up his strength he learned how to wrestle. Soon he could down the other pages, many of whom he had known in Warsaw at school. Then he was matched with the older guards.

For the next few months Casimir was as happy as a lark. There was so much new to see and learn that he had little time to be lonely. Then one morning he awakened to a terrific commotion. During the night, without warning, the Russian Army had surrounded the walls and laid siege to the castle. The Russian general, who had orders to force out the young Duke without violence if possible, had cut off all supplies coming from Warsaw. The Duke had only a handful of troops and boy pages. He was helpless.

When the news reached Warsaw, Count Pulaski urged the King and the nobles to send an army to the relief of Courland. Instead, the King sent a commissioner to study the situation. In the report he sent back the commissioner asked for two thousand troops. The King sent only forty men. As the weeks slid by Casimir had an opportunity to observe the Russian Army organization and its tactics.

Though he was but fifteen, the Duke did not hide his perilous situation from his page. In turn Casimir was outraged by the humiliating treatment the Duke received from the Russian commander.

Back in Warsaw Joseph Pulaski was unable to persuade the King and the nobles to mount an army. The King said, "What is the use in going to war for Courland? Courland is too small and unimportant. Besides, it must be disagreeable for the Russians to have a Polish fort on their frontier."

The advisors of the King made the same reply, adding, "It is better to cede Courland to Russia than to provoke a war."

The Duke of Courland received orders to hand over his castle to the Russians and to return to Warsaw with all his belongings. Casimir was embarrassed for his country. Poland had met defeat. In those days everyone, even the peasants, called Russia "that old woman"—so weak and impotent was she thought to be.

As Casimir traveled back to Warsaw with the Duke and his retinue at the head of their train of baggage wagons, the peasants they passed along the road lowered their heads in shame or made the sign of the cross to show their silent understanding of the disgrace. It was the first time in all history anyone had taken over Polish land without the firing of a shot.

During the six months Casimir had been away from home he had changed from a boy to a man. His experience in Courland imprinted indelibly on his mind the weakness of compromise. This retreat he foresaw was only the prelude to further disaster because those in authority had opened the way to surrender of their rights.

When the weary procession wound over the bridge and up the cliff into Warsaw, Casimir said good-bye to his beloved Duke and Duchess and galloped ahead to his father's house. There were tears of shame in his eyes as he threw himself into Count Pulaski's arms, his last boyish display of emotion.

He found his father in a somber mood. Joseph Pulaski could not work at his law practice when he, too, foresaw that his country would be gobbled up bit by bit by the Russians if nothing were done. He decided to go home and invite all those who felt as he did to hold a council at Winiary.

Scarcely had father and son reached home when they received word of the death of the King. This was the moment for which many were waiting: to hold a Diet and choose a new king. Of course Joseph and his friends hoped to force the election of the young Duke of Courland.

Packing his coach, Joseph and his three sons set out at once for the capital. As they approached the city, they joined the stream of 35,000 electors coming from every part of Poland. The dust on the highway was so thick they could hardly breathe in the solid line of horses and carriages of all kinds loaded down with provisions for those prepared to camp in the fields outside Warsaw.

On the bluffs above the river a city of tents sprang up overnight. The sun rose upon thousands of bright banners, each decorated with its coat of arms fluttering in the morning wind. Here and there groups of people were shouting and gesticulating as they worked up to fever pitch their enthusiasm for the various candidates. Besides the supporters of the

Duke of Courland and those of Count Krasinski, father of the young Duchess, there was a powerful group backing Stanislaus Augustus Poniatowski, a poor member of one of the great princely families.

At noon there was a fanfare of trumpets. From all parts of the immense camp men on horseback converged on the vast square set aside for the election. Excitement mounted as the partisans of the various

claimants shouted and booed. Finally the President of the Diet called for order so that the voting could begin. As each name was called a horseman rode out to join the standard of his chosen leader. When the votes were counted, Poniatowski had won. Few realized that Empress Catherine of Russia, who was in love with him, had bribed many to give him their vote.

Poniatowski was an attractive young man; he was well educated and had traveled to all the capitals of Europe; he loved poetry and music. But he was a weakling and when, despite strong opposition, he was elected king, many patriotic Poles were dismayed, feeling that his reign would prove a disaster to their country. The story of the next ten years was to show their fears well founded.

3

The Knights

AFTER THE ELECTION Joseph Pulaski did not hide his disgust. He gathered his friends around him and set out for Winiary. Again the household bustled with preparations, and again the tables creaked and groaned under the load of dishes set upon it. But the guests were not smiling as they drank the toasts. Many schemes were discussed and plans made and unmade. But after several weeks they were unable to agree upon a line of action, and one by one the guests departed.

In Warsaw the Russian ambassador, Repnin, stealthily went to work, tightening still further the noose his country was slipping about the neck of Poland. He arranged for a bill to be introduced in Parliament making two religious parties where formerly there was but one, united with Rome. The effect of the new law actually gave the Eastern Orthodox population a privileged position. The country was electrified at this proof of the power of Russia to dominate the internal affairs of the Polish nation. Little did they realize that the law was a trap set to catch them in a way they least suspected. Knowing the loyalty of the Poles to their bishops and to the Roman Catholic Church, the Russian ambassador whispered in the ear of one of the most outspoken, "Why don't you hold a Diet and protest the law?"

When Joseph Pulaski heard a Diet was to be held to censure the King he hurried to the meeting. This conclave was held outside Warsaw and was well attended. It was voted unanimously that the Roman Catholic Church and her laws were supreme in the land.

As soon as the vote had been taken, Repnin hastened to inform the British, Germans, Swedes and Dutch that Poland was planning religious persecution, and immediately all the Protestant and Orthodox nations in Europe sent letters of protest. Thus by accusing her of religious intolerance, the wily Russian ambassador isolated Poland. In the meantime he had his puppets in the Warsaw

Parliament denounce the separate Diets as groups of hotheaded revolutionary traitors and to beg the Russian Army to come into Poland to protect the Orthodox population.

Too late Joseph Pulaski saw that he had played into Repnin's hands. Challenging him to a duel, he shouted, "You will see that the Polish people, who love their liberty, will oppose the Russian troops with their lives." He would have killed the ambassador on the spot had not his friends dragged him away.

Now at last the line of action was clear. A strong party developed in opposition to the King. Help was sought in France and Austria, the natural enemies of the Russians.

Early in 1767 Joseph Pulaski, who during the sixty-four years of his life had never carried a gun except to shoot rabbits and birds, undertook to organize an army. He conceived of forming a military order like the crusading knights of old, each volunteer to pay his own expenses and use his own equipment. Calling themselves Knights of the Holy Cross, they would take vows like a religious order to serve Our Lord and His holy Mother until death, and never to marry until Poland was free.

The first Knights were Joseph's own sons and his son-in-law, for Josepha had married. By now

Casimir was nineteen, his elder brother Francis twenty-one, and little Anthony fourteen. The young Knights knelt in the family chapel and professed their solemn vows to Father Mark at the altar rail, while their mother, father and sisters prayed for their success.

Later that day, during dinner, Joseph explained his scheme for collecting arms and recruits without detection by the Russians. His estates, fortunately, were well scattered across Poland: Casimir would go east, Francis west, ostensibly to oversee them. Some of the farms could be used by his sons as bases where they could hide the arms and men they recruited. Other lands were to be sold and the money used to buy equipment for anyone who could not afford to pay for his own horse, lance or guns. Under the pretext of supervising Anthony's education, Count Pulaski would set up headquarters in Lwów where the family had many friends. Actually, Anthony was to go with him to serve as his page.

As soon as these decisions were reached, all prepared to leave at once. Little did the sons realize as they knelt for their mother's blessing next morning after breakfast that they would never see her again; nor their sisters nor their beloved Winiary. They rode down the lime-tree alley waving their hats in good-bye as gaily as they had done countless times before. They trotted through the village with its brightly painted houses, stopping to exchange good wishes with the peasants. Frost sparkled like diamonds in the early morning sun, whitening the northern bark of the trees. The air was sharp and clean, and the peat smoke rose in aromatic spirals to a clear blue sky.

Before they parted at the crossroads, Francis and Casimir watched their father's coach turn up the hill.

"Good luck," Casimir called nonchalantly, hiding the emotion which he felt.

"God keep you," Francis answered. "Please be careful. Remember the Russians are everywhere." Wheeling about, he set his horse into an easy canter and he, too, disappeared from view.

Despite Casimir's unhappy experience at the Duke's court, he had learned a great deal about the use of arms, and since his return to Winiary he had kept himself in training. For the past three years he had pored over books of history and descriptions of battles. All he had studied he now put into practice.

As soon as the new Knights enlisted, they were hidden on one of the Pulaski estates where Casimir began to drill and train them. His most valuable recruits were experienced officers who could be left in charge of a detachment while he rode away by night to the next place where he had friends.

Usually he was very well received. Occasionally, however, he would be told, "Do you realize you are proposing treason against the King?"

"Our country is in mortal danger," he would then try to explain.

The retort, "You will start by fighting the Russians but end up in a civil war," would make him feel like exploding.

"What makes people so shortsighted?" he thought to himself, managing to mask his temper but heartily wishing his diplomatic brother Francis were there to help.

Yet both their missions were a success. Within a year Francis had found several thousand nobles willing to give money and supplies. Casimir had collected an army, with officers to train it, and had kept them hidden from the watchful eyes of the Russians in small companies on his father's and neighboring farms.

The Pulaskis, father and sons, carried the entire burden of the movement, not only the financial responsibility but its diplomatic and military leadership as well. It was they who aroused the country to its danger, yet they realized that at any moment they could be handed over to the King as traitors.

Joseph Pulaski could not indefinitely hide his activities from the Russians in Lwów. He soon needed new headquarters. He moved to the little town of Bar because it was a secluded place far out in the country and famous for its shrine. Soldiers could be smuggled in disguised as pilgrims.

The detachments formed by Casimir arrived one by one at Bar until between five and six thousand troops were assembled. Then, with a fanfare of trumpets, Joseph Pulaski read a manifesto which he hoped would awaken the nation.

The manifesto called the whole world "to witness the obligation which bound the Poles to repel by arms, if need be, the foreign yoke placed on a free, independent nation by the Empress of Russia." It called on the whole nation "to arise, to postpone every other consideration but that of resisting tyranny."

The Knights who assembled at Bar all knelt together to pledge allegiance and took a vow to defend their country and the Catholic Church but never to persecute others because of their religion. Each wore the Holy Cross embroidered on his cap; his pay would be Christ's protection.

The commander in chief of the Knights was chosen by vote, the other officers by lot. Joseph urged them to elect Count Krasinski as civil and military commander. Naturally Father Mark was made the religious leader. The next days were spent in prayer and church processions, sermons and patriotic speeches. Casimir took to heart his vows as a Knight of the Holy Cross. He resolved that as long as he lived he would never again think of his own personal safety, comfort, or even life.

While all this was going on, other patriotic groups began forming in Warsaw and Cracow.

But whereas they waited for foreign aid to arrive before fighting, the Knights at Bar challenged the Russians to leave Polish soil at once or to bear the consequences.

The four Pulaskis were now in the saddle every day enlisting more recruits and gathering arms and money. Scattered throughout eastern Poland, detachments of the Knights were now openly trained, drilled, maneuvered. But they were still far from ready when the Russians sent 8,000 men in forced march to put down "this revolt against the King." All the supplies promised had not yet arrived, the soldiers were barely ready.

As the Russians drew near, Casimir went out with a company to scout their position. Unexpectedly he came upon the whole enemy army, and in a surprise attack he caught the Russians unaware. Running into the fire of Casimir and his men, the Russians thought they had met with the vanguard of a large force. Their commander sounded the bugle to retreat, and the Poles returned jubilant to Bar. From then on Casimir called himself "guerrilla colonel."

From his own experience he had found that guerrilla warfare, harassing the enemy with lightning raids when they least expected it, and then melting into the forest, was for the Poles the best method of pursuing the war. However, his opinion was not shared, and he was ordered to go to hold the ancient monastery fortress of Burdyczow where all the families backing the Knights had stored their gold and valuables. Despite his disappointment at the decision, he obeyed and took up his headquarters in the old Carmelite monastery within the fort.

This fort, now falling into ruin, had been built long ago on a high bluff above an almost circular loop in the river. Though impregnable from the three sides and protected by the river, it also provided no way of escape and Casimir soon realized his back was to the wall.

The Russians appeared and set up camp on the fields before the fortress. At first the Poles made audacious sorties and the battle went well for them. But the Russians could not only bring in new troops but cut off from the Poles all reinforcements and supplies sent from Bar. After two weeks water and food gave out in the fort and the monks begged Casimir to end the terrible slaughter and accept the honorable truce which the Russians were offering. Men who were dying from their wounds also begged him to give up.

Remembering his vows, Casimir preferred death to this. But he was barely twenty, and how could a youth of his age oppose the wishes of the Prior? The white flag was hoisted on the walls.

Casimir was forced to surrender. He, his brothers, and all the Knights at Burdyczow were imprisoned by the Russians. In one stroke their army with all its equipment, and the entire wealth of the nobles who had built it up, had been lost.

When the disastrous news reached Bar, Joseph Pulaski was told, "Your three sons have perished."

"I'm sure they did their duty," he replied calmly, and continued giving orders, for the Russians were now approaching Bar.

As the enemy came into sight Father Mark stood on the ramparts of the town holding a crucifix aloft. A Russian cannon fired at him but burst apart. This apparent miracle encouraged the inhabitants to send out of the city gate a procession of monks and surpliced priests to beg the enemy to retire. But immediately the Russians raked the priests with fire, mowed them down like grain, and stormed the town.

Seeing the hopelessness of their situation, Joseph and about two thousand elderly nobles of the Confederate Diets escaped over the Turkish frontier twenty miles away. But several more regiments of the Knights were captured.

The Polish King proclaimed the end of the "rebellion." The Russians were embarrassed as to what to do with the prisoners they held. Since their avowed purpose was to help the Polish King, they could not send Casimir and the other officers they had captured to Russia. They sent the troops home and kept the officers under guard.

People who had never heard of Casimir before began to call him a martyr. In vain the King boasted that the hotheads who might have brought about a war with Russia had been crushed. The longer Casimir and the other officers remained in Russian hands, the more unpopular the King became.

Meanwhile, the Russians tried to get Casimir to sign a pledge never to fight again, but each day his resolution not to sign grew stronger. He still felt he must keep his vow to die fighting for God and his country, and nothing could induce him to change his mind.

Neither the King nor the Russians wanted him to become a national hero. Finally, therefore, they banished him and his brothers over the Turkish frontier, warning them never to return.

In Turkey the sons found their father without too much difficulty. He scarcely gave them time to relate their adventures when he told them that despite all warnings he intended to return to Poland to renew the fight. Even then he was busy composing a new manifesto to the people.

They started out the following day and the minute they set foot on Polish soil, Joseph Pulaski issued a stinging proclamation in which he said, "The Russian language has no word for honor but many for fraud. As a people they can neither be disarmed by justice, mollified by submission nor surfeited by pillage!"

He told his sons to prepare new headquarters and to begin enlisting a new army while he himself would return to Turkey to rally the two thousand Confederates who had followed him into exile. Hardly had he recrossed the frontier when the Turks arrested him and threw him into prison!

Alone now, the three brothers resolved to carry out their father's plans. Francis, now twenty-two, was to explain their cause to the Polish people, find money and enlist recruits. Casimir, at twenty, aided by his younger brother Anthony, not yet sixteen, was to train the new army. They set up their headquarters in two old forts guarding both sides of the Dnieper River near the Turkish border.

Naturally the Russians heard about the troops and ammunition being gathered. But this time they told the Polish King that since the Turks had now declared war on Russia, they feared their enemy would invade Russia across Poland and that they must have strongholds on the Dnieper River to prevent this. The King agreed to let them have the very same two forts where the Pulaski brothers were established.

When the Knights learned that the Russians were approaching, Anthony begged to be allowed to reconnoiter their position. The boy was caught by the enemy, who, jubilant at having one of the Pulaskis in their hands, shipped him off to Siberia. Casimir and Francis were in despair at the loss of their beloved "little brother," and unable to learn of his fate, now mourned Anthony as dead.

The Russians laid siege to the old forts and set the roofs on fire. An old gypsy who knew a secret trail down over the slippery rocks to the river led the Pulaskis and their troops away at night.

Next morning the Russians found everyone gone. Because the river was flooded with swirling cakes of ice and some bodies of men and horses had been found washed up on the banks, they concluded that all the Knights had perished. They had certainly vanished completely.

After this escape from the fort Casimir suffered another blow. He became separated from Francis, and spent days searching for him. He was in despair. Could this brother, too, be lost? Yet he dared not stay where he was.

Casimir knew that although most of the population in the Warsaw provinces looked on the Knights as traitors, Cracow, far to the west, was alert to the growing menace of Russia. There the peasants and townsmen gave the gentry their loyal support, and there the Confederates of Bar were re-forming.

Casimir and his men decided to join the newly-formed forces at Cracow, but the Tatra Mountains lay between, their lofty pinnacles of ice and snow forming a natural barrier. Impassable in winter, in spring and summer the black ravines frothed with swirling cascades. Brigands lurked in the rocky caverns and chased the game out of reach of travelers whom they attacked and tried to kill.

Yet this was the only route open to Casimir and his Knights if they wished to reach Cracow. They had grown up on the sunny open plains and had no experience of climbing through rocky terrain. During this march three quarters of their forces died of hunger, exposure and wounds received in battles with the brigands. Less than a hundred ragged, half-starved men survived to reach Cracow. They looked like a band of beggars as they limped into the city.

Still, at last they were among friends where they could sleep in peace and nurse their wounds.

Casimir immediately sought out the leaders of the Polish Revolutionary Confederates.

"I will serve you as a common soldier if God and the best interests of Poland demand it," he said. "Do not think I am seeking honor or titles, but the freedom of my country."

The leaders were impressed with his sincerity, but they felt that he was too young and impetuous to be given a position of command. Although they were opposed to the King's policy of permitting Russian troops on Polish soil, they did not wish to start a civil war. They themselves were trying to frighten the Russians away by making an alliance with France. However, Radziwil, a powerful prince, and several realistic nobles gave money to Casimir to reoutfit the Knights.

He had made many new recruits when news reached Cracow that Francis had escaped to Turkey. He had been trying to free his father from prison and was planning to return to Poland in his company. Casimir and his forces set off at once to join his brother. His troops, now hardened mountaineers and better equipped, quickly recrossed the Tatras, this time making the long journey without loss.

As they finally descended to the plains, their scouts reported the movement of unknown soldiers.

Not knowing whether they were friend or foe, Casimir had just ordered his men into battle position when with a shout he recognized Francis and joyously flung himself into his brother's arms.

"Where is our father?" was Casimir's first question.

Francis looked down, his face torn with grief. He was scarcely able to speak but finally he said, "Our father is dead."

"God and all the saints protect us!" Casimir stammered. "When did this happen?"

"It was in Turkey about three months ago," Francis explained. "Every day I went to the Pasha trying to find out why they were holding our father. I was shunted from one government office to another. At last I heard a rumor that plague had broken out in the prison where he was. I begged the Turks to move him out of the common dungeon where he was being held. You never saw such a foul, dirty, such an evil-smelling place! Father knew he would never get out alive. Before his death he begged me to leave him, get my men out of Turkey and go back to Poland to fight. Neither of us imagined you were still alive."

"Surely you didn't leave his body there?" Casimir demanded.

"No, we loaded his coffin on a gun carriage and covered it with the banner of the Knights," Francis replied. "As I could not find a priest in Turkey, we planned to bring him back to Winiary for burial. Scarcely had we crossed the Polish frontier when the Russians pounced upon us. All my men were weary and sick from their wounds, and we were outnumbered. When the Russians refused to allow us to proceed with the coffin we had to surrender it and our poor father's body was left on the open prairie."

Casimir was too stunned by the horrible details of his father's death to hide his emotion. Nor was he ashamed of the tears which were shared by many of his loyal followers as both companies of soldiers mingled to recount their sad adventures. Francis led the way back to his headquarters in the ancient city of Sambor. Here the banners of the Knights wound about with black streamers hung from the windows of the fine old churches. The townsmen greeted the brothers with signs of sympathy and thronged the churches where requiem masses were said for the repose of the soul of the noble patriot Joseph Pulaski.

4

The Polish Confederates

AFTER THE LAST RESPECTS had been paid to their father, the brothers longed to return to Winiary and console their poor mother and sisters. But on his deathbed Joseph Pulaski had urged a new campaign. He had begged his son not to waste time going home but to use all his time and strength in reorganizing the shattered Polish forces.

Obedient to his final wishes, the brothers decided upon a plan of action. Leaving most of their troops in Sambor, Francis and Casimir went north to Lithuania which now suffered from Russian occupation. There the population was intensely anti-Russian and was ripe to start an organized revolt. Wherever the Pulaskis traveled they found friends and loyal support. Francis knew how to present their plans, and new recruits rallied to their side.

Four thousand well-equipped men volunteered to serve under Casimir's command. He taught them all the elements of guerrilla warfare, all the tactics he had learned through painful experience. Throughout the summer his troops were able to cut to pieces small detachments of the enemy and acquired huge stocks of arms and ammunition. At last they were powerful enough to engage the main Russian army massed in Lithuania, and on July 6, 1769, at the battle of Kukielki, they forced it to retire.

Now for the first time since King Stanislaus Poniatowski came to the throne there were no Russian troops in Poland, and for the next months there was actually the peace of which the King had never tired of speaking. Casimir had become the national hero overnight, and the Confederates made him their commander in chief.

But Catherine the Great did not sit idly by. She ordered the general of all the Russian armies to mobilize her country in a new campaign against Poland. More than 10,000 men were hired, trained and ordered to Lithuania to encircle the army of Pulaski. As the Russians approached, Casimir drew them into a vast swamp from which there was no retreat. His infantry, placed in hiding, cut them to pieces, leaving only scattered detachments of a weakened enemy roving the country in an effort to regain the Russian frontier.

Casimir and Francis decided that this was a good moment to return to Sambor to collect the forces they had left behind there, in order to unite them with the Polish armies in Lithuania. Prince Sapieha, a nobleman of the country, was placed in charge of those left behind. The Prince begged the brothers to return swiftly, and rather than travel through the swamps and woods as they had come, to take the open road.

"You don't need to worry about the Russians," Sapieha insisted; "they are licking their wounds."

Against their better judgment the brothers set out through open country, Francis galloping at the head of the little company and Casimir bringing up the rear. One day, when they were over halfway to Sambor, Francis was hailed by two men who courteously begged him to halt. He quickly reigned in his horse, not realizing the men were Russians in disguise.

"Your brother has been captured," they told him. Unsuspecting of the trick, Francis turned back and was quickly surrounded by a detachment of Russians who led him blindfolded to their general.

In the meantime Casimir, who had seen the enemy approaching, shouted to his men to scatter under cover, and thus he escaped capture. Hiding in the neighborhood, he spent days searching for Francis, but he never saw his brother again. Some peasants told him that Russian soldiers had sold a bloodstained uniform in their village and boasted that their general had killed Francis Pulaski, hacking him to pieces with his very own sword. This ghastly news, following the terrible circumstances of his father's end, would have crushed a lesser man.

And more sad news was to reach him before long. A remnant of the Russian Army had swooped down on Winiary to wipe out every trace left of the Pulaski family. The manor house and farm buildings were burned to the ground, but fortunately Countess Pulaska and her daughters managed to get away in disguise. Not knowing this, Casimir now believed that all his family were dead and that he alone remained.

It was not until a year later that he learned his mother and sisters had escaped and that Anna had carried out her childhood intention of becoming a nun. Five years were to pass before the news reached him that Anthony had finally been freed from Siberia.

During the six months following Francis' death Casimir renewed his forays against the Russians, using Sambor as his headquarters. Men flocked to fight under his banner, and he was so successful that Empress Catherine of Russia issued an order that anyone caught helping him would be punished. To carry out this command, the Russian commander chopped off the hands of a dozen peasants suspected of giving aid to Pulaski and sent them to Warsaw as a warning.

Not wishing to bring such suffering upon the local population, Casimir decided, in August, 1770, to leave Sambor and go to Cracow, where he had news that the Confederates were at last willing to go on the offensive. For the past two years they had been waiting for France to send them military aid, and at last it was rumored to be on its way.

Shortly after Pulaski reached Cracow the long-awaited French General Dumouriez and his staff arrived in Poland. Although the general brought no troops or supplies he was greeted with joy by the whole city which believed that a French army was to follow him. The leaders of the Confederates immediately submitted all their plans to General Dumouriez, and Casimir was among those who had a conference with him.

He found that the French general had no idea of Polish topography or the kind of warfare best suited to harass the enemy. Instead, he proposed a grandiose scheme for occupying a chain of defensive fortresses. To this Pulaski objected that he had obtained better results with offensive warfare, and that the guerrilla tactics he had developed over the past two years had been the cause of his success. A heated discussion took place. After the meeting was over, General Dumouriez wrote home, "I have met Pulaski, a mere rascal of a fellow and a bandit. I will have no use for his services. He knows nothing about military strategy."

The Confederates backed the French plan. Had they stood behind Pulaski, the outcome of the war would have been very different. Unfortunately, they listened to arguments concerning his youth and rashness, and he was ordered to obey the French general. It was decided that he should be placed in command of the ancient convent-fortress of Częstochowa.

Reluctantly Pulaski set out from Cracow for Częstochowa. He could hardly refuse to make his headquarters at this famous place for down the

centuries it had been known as the rallying place of all Poles. Here a picture of Our Lady, said to have been painted by St. Luke, was believed to have saved Poland at other momentous moments of its history. He knew, moreover, that the Romanesque church and monastery were built on a hill, surrounded with heavy walls and a wide moat, and could be strongly defended on all sides. But he also heard the unhappy monks there were praying for peace and did not want their shrine to be at the center of the coming battles.

Before Pulaski reached his new post and while Częstochowa was still unprotected, the Russian Army arrived. The peasants from the neighboring farms and the citizens of the town put up such determined resistance that the Russian general saw he could not take the fort peacefully. He then demanded an enormous sum in ransom, as well as all the fabulous jewels and votive plates of the shrine.

Fortunately, Casimir was not far away when this news reached him. He made a surprise attack and the Russians hastily withdrew. Although the monks were saved, they would not open the gates to his troops, and Pulaski was far too devout to force an entrance. However, he learned that the papal nuncio was staying in the monastery for the feast of the Coronation of Our Lady to which many pilgrims were coming from all over Poland. So he asked that his men might enter as pilgrims and receive the blessing of the nuncio.

The monks could not refuse. When they saw how truly anxious Pulaski was to protect their hallowed shrine, and how truly pious and devout he was, they threw their arms about him and allowed him to make Częstochowa his headquarters.

Soon after he was established the Duchess of Courland entered into Casimir's life once more. She had never lost her faith in him and she arranged for him to meet General Zaremba, who had been one of the best-trained officers in the King's army. This general had broken with the King for permitting the Russian Army to remain on Polish soil, and he now became Pulaski's ally. Zaremba understood the danger of keeping the Confederate forces locked up in the fortress of Częstochowa, and he and Pulaski agreed upon a plan to draw the Russian Army away to Poznań, far to the west, in order to give Casimir the much-needed time to organize his defenses. At Poznań, Zaremba inflicted enough damage on the Russians to cause them to turn to the Germans for help. Since Częstochowa was their real objective, they asked for the newest cannons and the gun crews to man them, for they would need these modern weapons to break through the heavy walls of the fortress.

From Cracow, General Dumouriez, instead of sending troops and supplies for the defense of the monastery, dispatched a few staff officers to Częstochowa to order Pulaski about. They found him in a fever of preparations, for the enemy was coming closer every day. He had melted the lead tiles to make cannon balls, and in their place covered the roofs with clay and manure to make them fireproof.

Outmoded guns were being repaired, and crews of soldiers were carting food from the countryside. Prudently Casimir kept much of his cavalry outside the fortress to harass the enemy and bring in reports of its movements.

The Russians, reinforced by the Germans, began moving in with tremendous force for the battle. They put the new German cannons in position, and on New Year s Day, 1771, began blasting at the walls. Casimir placed all his hope in Our Lady; the day before the battle he spent hours on his knees begging for her intercession, and that morning all his men went to Communion. Every time a German cannon ball bounced off the parapets he would cry out exultantly that God was with his little band.

After four days it was clear that the Russians were not going to make a dent in the defenses. At night Casimir would creep outside the fortress with a few intrepid soldiers, cut down the sentries, and overturn the German-operated gun emplacements. During the day the cavalry he had kept outside the walls would suddenly gallop up to the enemy's rear lines and catch them in the cross fire, while the soldiers inside Częstochowa strafed the Russians with bullets.

Then the Russians seized Polish peasants to use as shields for the attacking troops who were to mount scaling ladders on the walls. Wave after wave were ordered to take the place of those mowed down. Any Russian soldiers who reached the ladders were hurled to death by heavy stones rolled down on their heads from above. Casimir was everywhere at once, urging his men to redouble their efforts. More than 1,500 Russians died in the moat alone. The branches with which the poor peasants had been ordered to hide the troops were set on fire, making a blazing inferno around the whole fortress. Even the shells glancing off the wall did more harm to the Russians below than to the Poles.

At last the Russian commander saw it was useless to send more men to their death. When the Polish cross fire endangered his own staff, he gathered what remained of his army about him and fled.

Until the Poles had time to go over the field they could not believe the extent of their victory. They found more uniforms and arms than could be used by their entire army. Pulaski was the man of the hour. The papal nuncio sent him his blessing. The kings of Sweden, Austria, Saxony and Prussia and the leaders of other European countries expressed their admiration. But Catherine of Russia, smarting under the blow, made new plans, this time more subtle, to destroy the Polish hero. These she communicated to her ambassador in Warsaw.

Now even the Confederates, who had wavered before, urged that Pulaski be made commander in chief of the Polish forces. But General Dumouriez would not consider it. Should the appointment be made, he said, the French would withdraw their alliance. "Pulaski may be courageous," he agreed, "but a twenty-four-year-old youth lacks the experience to be given supreme command." Dumouriez urged the Poles to choose, instead, a certain Count Potocki. He made this choice because he knew Potocki would do as he was told, and Pulaski had shown far too much independence.

Without in any way intending to aid the enemy, the French general played into its hands by fatally dividing the Poles at the very moment when unity could have saved the country. It was his idea to depose the King, and he helped draw up a proclamation to this effect. Some of the Confederates agreed with him, but he alienated those who, like General Zaremba, would fight the Russians but feared anything that might lead to a civil war. In backing Count Potocki as supreme commander of the Polish Army, Dumouriez kept arms and supplies from Pulaski as commander of the only active and experienced force in the field.

Many Poles hesitated, wondering whether to follow Pulaski. Then, because very few men volunteered for the army of Potocki, Dumouriez hired German and Austrian mercenaries. Thus the other two enemies of Poland were invited by him to enter the country.

In the meantime the Russians marched on Cracow where General Dumouriez had massed the French supplies. Their victory was swift and overwhelming. The army under Count Potocki was annihilated and General Dumouriez barely managed to escape with his life. The whole stockpile of French war matériel, so desperately needed by the Poles, was captured.

When the news of his defeat in Cracow reached France, Dumouriez was recalled. Back home he blamed the fall of Cracow on the Poles, accusing them of being so hopelessly divided that it was useless for France to continue her help. He tried to create the impression in France that Pulaski was a brigand surrounded by a handful of bandits, a worthless outlaw respected by none.

In Warsaw, the Russian ambassador was telling the Polish King the same story. He urged King Stanislaus to use his own personal troops to restore order. He assured him that her Imperial Highness Empress Catherine had no other object in sending her army into Poland than to help him keep his throne and stamp out the rebellion headed by the bandit Pulaski. Of course, the ambassador said, as soon as peace was restored to the kingdom, her men would be recalled. But the King, too, hesitated to start a civil war.

However, an incident now took place that convinced the King that Pulaski was his deadly enemy. Although Casimir was in no way responsible, it led to his loss of reputation and to his total undoing.

One night, as the King was returning to his palace, a group of masked men challenged his guard and shot one of his coachmen. At first stunned by amazement, the King, looking out of the coach windows, tried to identify the assailants in the darkness. That very evening the Russian ambassador had been telling him of the dangers he ran from Pulaski and the King thought at first that it was his great opponent. Then he recognized the leaders of the kidnaping party as two members of the Cracow Confederates who had signed the proclamation ordering him to abdicate.

When he was commanded to leave his coach the King meekly stepped out, mounted the horse held ready for him, and followed his captors. They led

him cross country and into the woods where they lost their way. Fearing pursuit and expecting to be caught at any moment by the royal guard, the kidnapers stumbled about becoming hopelessly lost and the King's horse broke a leg jumping a ditch. When this happened and he dismounted, the monarch realized where he was, for he had hunted in this forest many times.

As a fresh horse was being led up for him to mount, he demanded of the leader of the band, "Were you not one of those who swore allegiance to me seven years ago?"

The young Confederate officer agreed that he was.

"I see you have scant respect for your oath. You should be shot for treason, but accompany me to the convent of Mariemont and I will forgive you," the King commanded. He well knew that a direct road ran back to Warsaw from that point.

It was the King himself who led his captors out of the wood. One of them actually rode back with him to his palace in the capital. Here, the main body of the royal guard, unaware that the King was even missing, could hardly believe the story.

As he recounted his adventure, Poniatowski became more convinced than ever of the dangers he had escaped. He gave out that he had foiled a well-laid plan of assassination. When news of the affair was communicated to the courts of Europe, Frederick of Prussia wrote to congratulate the King upon his escape. "A plot so horrible and atrocious covers the Confederates with shame. All the countries in Europe should unite to take vengeance on the crime."

Though he knew very well that Pulaski had not been present, this was the pretext for which Poniatowski had been waiting to destroy the defender of Częstochowa. In his replies to the various kings of Europe, each letter was suited to the recipient. To the Pope he wrote, scolding the papal nuncio for giving his blessing to a murderer. He complained to the French King for sending arms to the aid of a brigand. He begged the Emperor of Austria and the King of Prussia never to let the "regicide" find asylum in their lands. To be called "regicide," or killer of a king, was a hundred times more dishonorable than to be called a murderer, and this false charge plagued Pulaski until his death.

The King was happy. Peace, he thought, was now assured. Had not the Russians promised to leave Poland as soon as Pulaski was silenced? To call him a "regicide" was to dishonor him in the eyes of all Poles and the rest of Europe. No one would lift a finger to help him now.

At Częstochowa, Casimir was horrified when he heard of the attempt on the King. General Dumouriez and the Confederates had often tried to persuade him to march on Warsaw and capture Stanislaus Augustus. Although he knew the King's weakness was the reason for the presence of the Russian troops on Polish soil, he had always refused to take any part in plans to remove the monarch by force. Even more he had opposed with all his strength any idea of assassination. "Poland," he had often boasted, "is the only country in Europe that in all her history never killed a king."

The Confederates who had actually made the plans to capture the King now burned all their letters and correspondence. They willingly let Pulaski take the blame rather than have it fall upon themselves.

As the monarch had expected, from one day to the next Casimir found himself shunned as a would-be murderer. He had taken no part in the plot and did not even know who was involved in it. But it was his word against the King's. To clear his name, Casimir wrote the King of France, "Though His Majesty sprinkled his throne with the blood of my relatives, I would die of despair had I conceived the idea of staining my sword by the murder of an enemy whom I could conquer honorably."

Many in France still had faith in Pulaski, but the Russians, Prussians and Austrians were given the pretext for which they had been waiting. Secretly they agreed to partition the country between themselves. For some time they had been seeking an excuse for this action. Now they moved swiftly. The Russians captured one Polish leader after the other and deported them to Siberia. Then they turned on General Zaremba in Poznań, caught him off guard, and chopped his troops to pieces.

At last the Poles saw the danger to their country. Armed as best they could, they rushed to join Pulaski at Częstochowa. Never had such great numbers rallied about him, never had he had such stock piles of arms. His was the only fighting force in the country. But from three sides the enemies were converging. The Austrians occupied all the Cracow provinces,

Frederick II of Prussia seized the Baltic provinces as well as the parts of the country bordering on Germany. Russia occupied the Ukraine, Lithuania and the eastern districts.

The position of the Polish troops at Częstochowa was hopeless. They could fight to the last man, to the last bullet, but they could receive no reinforcements and no help from outside the fortress. The entire country was under the control of foreign troops. What was Casimir to do? Should he ask so many young men, the flower of the nation, to give up their lives in vain? And the beautiful shrine, should he be the one to cause its total destruction? These were the questions he asked Our Lady as he knelt all night before her image and prayed.

He saw clearly that the superior forces pitted against him must eventually win unless the King rallied the country to come to their defense. But the King who had blackened Pulaski's reputation was convinced that the best way to keep peace was by refusing to fight and would not change his mind now. No, the King would not move. All the Confederate leaders were captured or in exile. Should the French send help, it would be stopped in Danzig.

The whole terrible decision would have overwhelmed a man without Pulaski's faith. He called his most trusted friends and told them to send home the troops with their arms to await a more propitious opportunity to free their country. Before dawn, June 1, 1772, he slipped out of the fortress, and in disguise left Poland never to return.

The astonished garrison awakened in the morning to learn the news of their leader's departure. The men wept bitterly when the farewell orders of their beloved commander were read: "I took up arms for the public good. For that same good I must lay them down. I do not want you to become linked with my misfortune. I know your courage, and know one day you will be able to display your zeal for your country again."

Poniatowski was jubilant when he learned Casimir had left Poland. Secure in his beautiful palace, surrounded by the prosperous Warsaw provinces which the partitioning powers cleverly did not molest, he was unaware that his country, which for seven hundred years had been the greatest power in Europe, existed no longer. He continued his receptions and balls where gentlemen in glittering uniforms answered his toast "To Peace."

5

Exile and Prison

DURING THE SUMMER OF 1773, and in their absence, the trials of Pulaski and of the two Confederates who actually *had* tried to kidnap the King were held in Warsaw. All received the death penalty and were to be beheaded as soon as they could be caught. Their bodies were to be burned after being exhibited to the public ridicule, their ashes flung to the winds. Casimir was now not only discredited, but he had been condemned to death as a regicide. He could never return to his country, and all his property had been confiscated.

In hiding, traveling by devious roads, he reached Dresden where the Duke of Courland was living. The King's accusation had preceded him and had destroyed the Duke's confidence, but out of loyalty to his former page he promised not to return him to Poland. Still Pulaski felt unsafe. He begged to be allowed to proceed to France and persuaded the Duke to write asking for asylum to be given him there. Weeks dragged by. There was no reply to the Duke's letter.

Casimir, who had shown such courage during five years of constant battles, then fell ill from suspense and inactivity. When he recovered, he took the assumed name of Rudzinski and went north to watch the maneuvers of the Prussian Army and learn their new methods of warfare. For three days he stayed at the camp, but when he was recognized, he fled. But the King of Prussia made no effort to pursue him as the King of Poland had requested.

Finally Casimir reached the French frontier, where he learned that King Louis XV had lost interest in helping Poland save to the extent of trying to make peace between Poniatowski and the Confederates. Still Casimir felt he would be safe in France, so he crossed the border. There he tried to join the French Army but was refused. No matter how hard he tried to clear his name, no one believed him. For a whole year he wandered about from one place to another. No one wanted to have anything to do with him.

In the autumn of 1773 news reached France of the defeat of a Russian army by the Turks. Casimir was again filled with hope. Among the Cracow Confederates who had escaped to Paris there was talk of a new war for restoring Polish freedom, and they pictured to the French the advantages to be gained by joining them. Victory over the common enemy should not be difficult, they said, while the Russians were engaged in fighting the Turks. Little did they know that the Ottoman Empire was soon to fall to pieces!

The group around Pulaski worked night and day to find recruits and supplies. They were assured of success when Prince Radziwil, the richest of the Polish princes, put his enormous fortune at their disposal.

No sooner had the Prince Radziwil published his intentions than there arrived at his court a mysterious lady who undoubtedly was a Russian spy. She was so beautiful that the unsuspecting prince fell head over heels in love with her and forgot all about his promises to Pulaski. The lovely charmer needed jewels and fine clothes, and a handsome coach to ride in. It took no time at all for her to spend all the money Radziwil had pledged to the Confederates.

Casimir knew nothing of all this. He had gone on to Venice where, on April 9, 1774, a rendezvous of French and Polish officers took place and where the expedition set sail. It consisted of a group of about seventy-five officers who would form the staff of a new Polish Army to be recruited when they reached Polish soil.

Begun in the highest of hopes and spirits, this expedition was destined for a disastrous end. Landing in Turkey, the party was warmly welcomed by the Sultan's representative and given a thousand horsemen, but to reach Southern Poland they had to pass over one mountain chain after another, and it took two months of incredible hardship to arrive at Jeni Pazar on the Turkish border. Here the final battle of the Russo-Turkish War was being waged. Casimir saw at once that the Turkish forces were in a hopeless position. The Poles watched as the Russians encircled the Turkish cavalry and charged. Suddenly the whole Turkish Army was in rout. The soldiers fell over one another trying to retreat, and one of their number slashed Casimir from his horse and stripped him of his baggage, money and identification papers.

The Polish officers were left in a desperate situation. They were alone, without friends or credit, in a hostile and defeated land. They knew they had to act quickly before the Russians caught them. They set off at once on foot for Adrianople where they hoped to find protection in the French Embassy. Yet the route to Adrianople led them still farther away from home.

Twenty-five of the officers were caught and imprisoned, others became too ill to travel. A small group of only seven finally reached their destination. Two French officers offered to beg the French ambassador to arrange for their return passage to France. One of them soon returned and insisted that Pulaski sign a check for the money which the Confederates had put into a French bank for the expenses of the expedition. He did so, and the officer left. He did not come back, and after a few days it became clear the man had stolen the money and fled with his companion. The French ambassador refused to receive Pulaski and the officers who remained with him. Every minute Pulaski remained in Adrianople increased the danger of their being caught and turned over to the Russians.

Dressed in Tartar costumes, Casimir and five companions set off for Constantinople, but there, too, no help was found no matter where they turned. When they heard rumors that the Russians would not sign peace with Turkey unless Pulaski were given up, they stole down to the harbor and boarded a small fishing boat in which they escaped to Smyrna.

Here at last they found friends who bought passage for them on a boat bound for Marseilles. The boat was leaving at once, and none too soon. Scarcely had it cleared the breakwater when a Russian man-of-war hove into sight. It was coming for Pulaski, but its captain, of course, did not know that Casimir and his friends were aboard the other ship until he reached Smyrna. By then six hours had been lost. Although the Russians set sail at once, they were unable to overtake the boat, and Casimir and his friends landed safely in Marseilles.

The French government permitted Pulaski to remain in Marseilles on condition he change his name and live very quietly. This was hard, but it was still harder to have nothing to do. He was twenty-seven years old, absolutely penniless, with no one to help him. Prince Radziwil, who had been so enthusiastic for the plan to enter Poland through Turkey that he had guaranteed the cost of the expedition, now thought of nothing else than spending more money on the beautiful lady who had already cost him an immense fortune. Pulaski's other countrymen in exile in France would do nothing about paying his debts.

Casimir was so impoverished that he still wore the Tartar costume in which he had escaped from Turkey. He searched for work, but no one seemed to have anything for him to do. He felt responsible for the five friends who had stood by him so bravely and could not watch them starve, so he bought food on credit, promising the shopkeeper to repay them when he received the money he was owed. The French government would not prosecute the French officer who had robbed them of their funds. Prince Radziwil did not reply to his letters. Weeks became months while the debts became greater, not only because of the high interest rate charged against the cost of outfitting the expedition to Turkey, but for the daily meager subsistence of the little group of officers.

No one had use for Pulaski's services. The disaster in Turkey seemed to have destroyed what was left of his reputation. Again he tried to enlist in the French Army but was refused because of his false reputation as a "regicide." No one answered his letters. Everyone tried to forget him. It seemed as though this was the end of his career.

Then one day as he was out strolling in the sun the police arrested him because of his debts and locked him in the deepest dungeon of Marseilles. Here the most desperate characters were kept. The inmates were ragged, filthy creatures loaded with heavy chains who roared and cursed by day and night. Debtors generally had more decent quarters, and his followers begged the authorities to move him. The tone of the prison keeper's "no" sounded as if he were acting on special orders.

Immediately the five friends broadcast all the facts: Pulaski had spent his own fortune in Poland to provide for the army fighting under Confederate orders. His present debts had been incurred outfitting an expedition on which the Confederates hoped to ride back to power.

Since his imprisonment was truly a disgrace to the Poles, the Confederates felt properly shamed. One by one they sent the money needed for his release. After a month spent in that deep, foul dungeon Casimir stepped out into the sunshine which he had given up hope of ever seeing again.

6

The American Dream

THE SHOTS that rang round the world in April, 1775, at the Battle of Bunker Hill had been fired just before Casimir was clapped into prison. Before his imprisonment he had been thinking about the brave Americans who were risking their lives for freedom, and wondering if he could not throw in his fate with theirs.

Now that he was free again, Pulaski read in newspapers about the Boston Tea Party, how the British had sent troops to put down the rebellion, and of the battle at Lexington. All his sympathies were with the Americans. In his own country the King was still talking about peace and working agreements with the partitioning powers. Casimir had tried, through his sister Anna, now a nun in a convent outside Warsaw, to have the court order rescinded, but the King was determined that the hotheaded warmongering Pulaski should never step foot on Polish soil again.

So after three years in exile Casimir was still unable to go home. He had the choice of either joining the exiled Confederates who lived in a dream world trying to get France, Switzerland and Germany to put political pressure on the Polish King to abdicate, or else of going to America to fight for the freedom of another downtrodden people.

His heart burned for the American colonists. He well understood the feelings of those willing to sacrifice everything for the freedom of their land. The more he thought about it, the more he longed to go to the colonies. But how could he get there? His debts were now paid but he had no money to buy passage. He could not go to Paris and see the American minister because at any moment he might be caught and handed over to his enemies.

Each day he went down to the wharves on the Marseilles water front where ships were being loaded with supplies for the American colonists. The boats carried the Spanish flag to protect them from capture by the British. As he watched the loaders straining under the weight of guns and ammunition, his determination to join the Americans grew. He knew the terrible mistakes of his attempt to reach Poland through Turkey had cost him the friendship of many Frenchmen who might have helped him now. He had to think very carefully of whom he would approach to introduce him to the American minister.

There was a very old and intimate friend of his father, now retired, called the Count de Rhulière. In times past he had visited at Winiary when he was staying in Poland to study conditions in that country for the French King. He was a member of the French Academy, a literary figure and a diplomat highly esteemed by his compatriots. He had watched the revolution in St. Petersburg which brought the German Catharine II to the imperial throne and had not hesitated to publish the facts about the assassination of Czar Peter III even though the Court of France did not wish those events made known.

In 1776 Rhulière had many friends in the French Ministry of Foreign Affairs. It was because of his defense of Pulaski that the French did not accept the story of the Russian ambassador or of the Polish King concerning the attempted "regicide." It was he who had arranged for Pulaski to live in Marseilles under an assumed name and had taken advantage of every possible occasion to praise his moral and military value.

It was therefore natural that Casimir should turn to the Count de Rhulière for help in approaching the American minister Benjamin Franklin. In reply Rhulière wrote that he had seen Franklin and that Casimir's petition had been granted on two conditions. First, no one in France or Europe should learn of his destination. Second, Casimir would have to pay his own way in America, but he could be given free passage on the next boat sailing from Brittany. Casimir had hoped to take his five friends from the Turkish campaign with him. This was refused.

America was flooded with so many adventurers that Franklin had been given strict orders to refuse all new applicants. On the other hand, Casimir was backed by the Count de Rhulière and others in the French Ministry of Foreign Affairs. He had by far the best military record of all the men who begged to be allowed to go to America. So Pulaski was given permission to come to Paris to be interviewed by the American minister.

From the moment he arrived in Paris, events moved swiftly. He was given a hero's welcome. All the great houses were opened to him; the term "regicide" seemed entirely forgotten.

Benjamin Franklin received Pulaski in the sumptuous little house in Passy which had been lent him by a French friend as a contribution to the success of the American mission. At seventy years of age he was the American best informed on the political questions of the day. He corresponded in nine languages, for he was immensely popular and had friends in all the European countries. His scientific writings had been translated into Italian, German and French and were widely read throughout the British Empire. It was for this reason that the Continental Congress had entrusted him with the supremely important mission of winning French aid for the colonists.

When Casimir was admitted into Franklin's presence he found a heavily built man with kind gray eyes, one heavily bandaged foot resting on a stool.

"So you want to join our fight," Franklin began directly in fluent French. "Please tell me, young man, why you want to go to America?"

Casimir answered without hesitation. "Sir, beyond everything I admire the Americans because they are willing to risk everything for freedom without waiting for foreign help. Without knowing whether they would ever receive aid they took up arms to preserve their own liberty."

Benjamin Franklin was pleased with this reply. "I hear you, too, are willing to take risks." He laughed. "You know the terms that have been proposed and that I can promise you nothing."

"Indeed, sir, I have written to my family asking for sufficient funds not to be a drain upon your expenses, and I will tell no one I am leaving," Casimir promised.

"Good, good!" Mr. Franklin said with a satisfied smile.

"I see, sir, you are ill," Casimir remarked.

"If gout may be called an illness," Franklin said. "I suspect it is a remedy. I find my health always improves after a fit of gout! I suffer chiefly from old age. I feel old age coming on so fast and this building so in need of repair that the Owner will soon find it cheaper to pull it down and build a new one."

Pulaski felt this was really a delicate hint and that he had already taken as much of the great man's time as he should. Thanking Franklin for receiving him, he made a sweeping bow and prepared to leave.

"I will send your letters of recommendation straight to our Congress, and another to General Washington to you at your hotel," Franklin promised, and with good wishes for a safe crossing, he said good-bye.

As soon as Pulaski left, the old man called for his writing case and composed a letter to General Washington. "Count Pulaski of Poland," he wrote, "an officer famed in Europe for his bravery in defense of the liberty of his country against the three powers, Russia, Austria and Prussia, will have the honor of delivering this to your Excellency's hands. The opinion here is that he may be highly useful to our Service."

The way was opening up for Casimir. Although his passage to America was provided for, he still had to equip himself, to reimburse the friends who had lent him money to go to Paris and to settle other debts he had made in Marseilles. In these matters he received help from some unexpected quarters. Certain persons in the Ministry of Foreign Affairs who, although he did not know it, were trying to patch up French relations with Russia, found it convenient to have Pulaski on the other side of the Atlantic. They were only too eager to find the money to help him prepare for the long voyage.

In addition Casimir's sister Anna, the nun, sent him 15,000 livres from the family funds, a huge sum of money with which he was to buy his equipment. Her letter contained the surprising news that at last his name had been cleared in Poland and that if he wished he would be permitted to return and live quietly in his own country.

But Casimir had chosen America and the fight for freedom. "I would rather," he told Count Rhulière, "live free, or die for liberty. I suffer more because I cannot avenge myself against the tyranny of those who seek to oppress humanity. That is why I want to go to America, otherwise I could live peacefully in Poland."

After making all his arrangements and gathering his letters of recommendation, Casimir said good-bye to his friends and set off for the seaport of Nantes where the SS *Reprisal* was waiting. This was the same ship on which Benjamin Franklin had come to France. It was loaded and ready to leave.

Although Casimir had tried to keep his movements as secret as possible, the British ambassador lost no time in writing to London: "The Americans have hired that assassin Pulaski." He even named the vessel on which Casimir was traveling and its destination. Since the British were trying to keep all reinforcements and supplies from reaching the colonists, this information greatly increased the danger of the *Reprisal's* voyage.

The *Reprisal*, disguised as a trading clipper, was actually the newest and finest battleship in the American Navy. It was heavily built of massive timbers and carried a heavy load of munitions hidden in its holds.

As Casimir stepped aboard, he felt the stout vessel under his feet solid as an oak. The captain bellowed, "Sails aloft!" and the ship rode out of the harbor into the open sea. A stiff head wind forced them off their course, and kept them out of reach of two British frigates waiting in the English Channel to pounce on them. The captain stationed his men at their battle posts, but they slipped into the dark vastness of the Atlantic without being molested.

Casimir was fascinated by everything aboard ship. He tried to learn the uses of the hundreds of ropes. Every time sails were reset he begged for an explanation. As he was the only passenger aboard, he spent hours with the officers and crew trying to learn the secrets of navigation which were completely new to him and the English language which he heard for the first time.

He was particularly astonished at the ship's provisions. Lettuce, radishes and other vegetables growing in boxes were placed in the lifeboats lashed on deck. Sheep, chickens and a few cows were penned amidships and sheltered from the wind by bales of hay secured by stout tarpaulins. If a storm broke out this stock of fresh food could easily be washed overboard and then everyone would have to eat salt pork and smoked fish from the barrels in the hold. Fortunately excellent weather held for the entire voyage.

The *Reprisal* had been at sea two weeks when the cry "Ship ahoy!" rang out from the crow's-nest. A clipper was seen heading in the opposite direction. The crew ran to man the guns, and the captain hoisted the signal to show colors. When the other ship ran up the American flag, the two vessels drew near enough to exchange news and a letter which Casimir had dashed off to his dear friend Count de

Rhulière. This was the only ship that was sighted until they reached American waters and the sole break in an otherwise peaceful trip.

But Casimir was never bored for an instant. Boats were an element in warfare he had never explored. He now realized how useful they could be in moving troops from one point to another to reinforce an army sent by land. During this trip he first had the idea, which never afterward left him, of a special branch of the Army like our present Marines, mobile because they moved on sea as well as land. He borrowed the captain's books on navigation and spent hours studying them.

While in his cabin he drew up campaign plans to present to General Washington in preparation for the moment when at last he would be face to face with this great man. Some of his ideas were impractical because he did not know American geography, but others showed his thoughtful common sense.

Every night he would kneel before a picture of Our Lady of Częstochowa painted in enamel on a tiny shield which he always carried with him. He beseeched the Holy Mother to guide him and to give a sign of approval to his mission. As a Knight of the Holy Cross he had always had a priest in his camp; now he feared he would be without one.

Since boarding the ship he had not been able to go to Mass. These things seemed to him a greater hardship than any he had experienced since he had accepted exile.

Our Lady must have quieted his fears because when at last the ship dropped anchor in Marblehead Bay in Massachusetts, he had joyfully resolved to accept whatever America held in store for him.

7

Washington's Aide

PULASKI REACHED BOSTON one hot July morning in 1777. The men working on the dock in their shirt sleeves grinned at the smartly dressed officer in his heavy wool uniform. He could not understand what they shouted at him but saluted smartly as he nimbly jumped on the wharf. The captain of the ship had promised to guide him to General Heath, commander of American forces in the city, and Casimir was eager to find him.

Casimir was now thirty years old with fourteen years of military experience. In Poland men had rushed to enlist under his banner, yet he knew that in America he would have to prove himself all over again. The hero's honors showered on him in Paris had not turned his head, and he was so anxious to start his military service that he hardly glanced about him as he threaded his way through the busy Boston streets.

General Heath was expecting him and greeted him warmly. He answered Casimir's questions in French, using a map to show the British moves in the campaign. Pulaski quickly realized he had arrived at the most critical moment of the Revolutionary War. The Americans were in a perilous position.

Part of the British Army under Lord Howe was sailing down the coast, to attack General Washington whose headquarters were in Philadelphia. General Burgoyne had just routed the Americans at Ticonderoga and captured all their guns and ammunition; at this very moment he was marching on Albany. There was nothing to stop his taking that city, joining forces with the British in New York and cutting the colonies in two.

General Heath invited Pulaski to stay with him while he was in Boston. His headquarters were established in a fine brick house, furnished in mahogany, the hangings in silk brocade. Dinner was set out with style, with good French wine served in crystal goblets. The appointments rivaled anything he had seen in Paris and made Casimir feel very much at home. Another time Casimir would have enjoyed such pleasant surroundings. Now, he was restless to reach General Washington as fast as possible.

After dinner General Heath showed him the fortifications around Boston, hoping he could persuade Casimir to remain with him. The fortifications were well manned and in excellent condition. But Casimir realized that the decisive battles would not be fought in Boston, and pleasant as it was there, he longed to be in the center of the conflict.

In those days it was a long journey on horseback from Boston to Philadelphia where Washington had his headquarters. General Heath helped Pulaski procure a horse and gave him detailed instructions where to cross the Hudson as well as a letter to General Washington. He bade him good-bye, not without expressing regrets at losing his services. The night before leaving Casimir sent a long letter to Count de Rhulière asking for cloth, buttons, braid, stockings with which to make the uniforms for the corps of soldiers he confidently expected to lead.

As he rode southward, the rich farms of New England reminded him of Poland. There were well-appointed inns where he spent the nights, but when he passed through the backwoods hamlets he could not help but think of the Russian log-cabin villages. Dogs growled and snapped at his heels, and swarms of dirty children ran out to watch him go by. At last he reached the Hudson River near Beacon where he found a man to ferry him across the river. Here the wild highlands reminded him of the foothills of the Tatra Mountains.

In the deep, cool ravines of the Catskills he felt safe. He could water his horse and relax. There were no British in the neighborhood, and the danger of meeting them on the Hudson River was passed.

The shaded mountain road finally led down to the Jersey plains scorching in the late August sun. He crossed the Delaware at Trenton, and when he reached Philadelphia he did not stop to join the festivities and the social gaieties of the city. Instead, he hurried straight to General Washington's headquarters, a few miles south on Neshanning Creek.

Of all the many letters of introduction he carried, none turned out to be so valuable as the letter from the wife of the Marquis de Lafayette. This was the first letter the young French twenty-year-old general had received from his beloved since his arrival in America, and immediately the two became fast friends. The Marquise de Lafayette had used glowing words in praise of the young Pole, and Lafayette used all his prestige with the Americans to help Pulaski. It was he who made the appointment for

Casimir to see General Washington and went with him as interpreter for their first meeting.

As Pulaski and Lafayette walked to General Washington's headquarters, Casimir appeared stiffly correct. Inwardly, however, he was bursting with excitement that at last he would meet the great commander whom he had traveled so many miles by sea and land to serve. He was about to offer Washington his unswerving loyalty and the American cause his life and fortune. He had dreamed of this meeting for so many months that he knew precisely what he intended to say.

General Washington had received glowing praise of the young Pole from Benjamin Franklin. He was anxious to meet this valuable and experienced officer who was coming to his aid at a moment when the Revolutionary Army was suffering so many serious reverses. George Washington greeted Pulaski warmly, expressing his gratitude with great sincerity.

Casimir presented the memorandum he had drawn up on shipboard and begged for a commission.

"Unfortunately," the commander in chief replied, "it is not in my power to grant your request. For that, the approval of the Continental Congress is needed."

This was a great blow to Pulaski. Like all men of action he was impatient and unable to wait calmly. It seemed a waste of time going back to Philadelphia to appear before the Congress. But he knew there was no time to be lost and so he returned to the city.

After he had delivered the letters Washington and Lafayette had given him, he sat down and wrote out an additional memorandum in such poor English that the Congressional Commission misunderstood him. They thought he was seeking command of the

Army rather than of the small independent cavalry corps he wished to recruit and outfit himself. When Congress sent him back to General Washington for more explicit orders, Pulaski wrote John Hancock, President of Congress, giving him further details of the "Vallenteur Corps" of two hundred officers and men he was proposing to form, to serve under the command of General Washington.

On his return to headquarters Casimir found that at the persuasion of General Lafayette, Washington had requested Congress to put Pulaski in charge of the American cavalry. In his letter he had pointed out that in Poland "the principal attention for some time past has been paid to the cavalry ... this gentleman is acquainted with it. I submit to Congress to confer the appointment I have mentioned. This gentleman, like us, has been engaged in defending the liberty and independence of his country and has sacrificed his fortune in his zeal for these objects."

Every day while waiting for his commission, Casimir rode out with General Washington to reconnoiter. One morning they learned that the British under Lord Howe were already in the Chesapeake. Two days later came news that the enemy had landed and were marching on Philadelphia. But still there was no news from Congress about

Casimir's appointment. Finally he could stand the suspense no longer. He galloped back to Philadelphia to learn whether he had received his commission. When he found it still had not been acted upon, he raced back to Washington's headquarters and offered to fight as a common soldier.

He had come to love the American Army, forced to organize in the midst of the enemy. The professional officers were criticizing Washington for his unorthodox methods, just as he himself had been criticized under similar conditions. Both men had learned in the hard school of experience. Both suffered from foreign allies who influenced the politicians behind the lines.

As Howe marched nearer, George Washington had withdrawn his troops north to Brandywine. Although he had asked that Pulaski be put in command of the cavalry, Casimir was alarmed to find the American commander himself actually not fully aware of the part cavalry could play in an offensive action. Mounted troops had been useless during the French and Indian Wars when guerrilla tactics were developed. Now that the Americans were faced with the conventional methods of a European-trained army, fighting in open country, they needed the greater mobility of cavalry. This was the chief weakness as Casimir saw it, but as yet he had not received a commission nor been able to give General Washington a practical demonstration of cavalry action.

He followed the general as an aide, admiring the courage of the ragged army with its assorted collection of firearms, the soldiers dressed in their own clothing of woodsmen or farmers. They reminded him of the Polish recruits he had led—volunteers filled with patriotism and with loyalty to their commanders. Whenever he heard the French sneer at the unpolished Americans, he remembered how Dumouriez had criticized the Poles.

One day while out scouting near Brandywine, Pulaski saw that the British were approaching very close. One column advanced out into the open, while the other, under Lord Cornwallis, was making a wide circle to reach the American rear. This was the kind of trap with which Casimir was very familiar. He reported at once to General Sullivan, who could not believe the news. The British struck, and the American Army was almost surrounded. General Lafayette was severely wounded, and a second French commander quit the battle in disgust. General Washington realized that the Army was in a desperate position and tried to save as much of it as possible by sending his supplies toward Chester. All hope was lost of saving Philadelphia, the capital.

This was the moment for which Casimir had waited to prove himself. He begged Washington to put him in charge of a small detachment of thirty cavalrymen. The right wing of the American Army was breaking, the center about to crack. Washington accepted at once.

As usual in battle Pulaski flew into the forefront of action and his companions followed at a gallop, leading a detachment of the troops General Washington had ordered to support him. They could scarcely understand his orders but his actions spoke clearly. The British, caught unaware, were halted. Even the foot soldiers about him rallied, and Washington had the needed time to save his supplies and extricate far more of his army than he had expected.

Casimir had proved the need for American cavalry. His gallant rear-guard action had saved for the moment the Revolutionary Army. Lord Howe decided not to pursue them further, since Philadelphia was in his grasp. He decided to make his triumphal entry into the city now and finish off the American forces later.

Pulaski was among the few men praised after the Battle of Brandywine. The American politicians blamed the officers for the defeat, the officers, one another. But everyone agreed that Pulaski had saved the day from complete disaster. The Continental Congress which had hesitated so long in giving him a commission that very day made him brigadier general in charge of cavalry. He had risked his life when he could have stood aside. He had shown a disinterested love of liberty. He had fought not for pay, or honors, but for freedom.

The night following the Battle of Brandywine, a full moon lighted the road as clear as day. Cool, fanning mists rose out of the hollows to soothe the fever of the wounded men jouncing in the hay of farm carts, and even those on foot marched more lightly.

Casimir overtook the retreating American Army before Chester. As he trotted up the line, he reined his horse to a slower pace. Filled with pity for the tired trudging men burdened by defeat, he longed to say some cheerful word of comfort. His English, unfortunately, was so poor that no one understood him. Then, suddenly, he noticed a French uniform. He slowed his horse to keep pace with the young officer.

"Greetings," Casimir called in French.

A tired young face smudged with smoke and grime grinned back at him in surprise.

"What are you doing here?" Casimir asked.

"I couldn't get a commission with the cavalry," the French officer explained, "so I signed up in the infantry under General Greene."

"What is your name?" Casimir asked.

"Lieutenant Paul Bentalou," the man replied. "I came over to help the Americans, so when I couldn't get in the cavalry, I took any job they would give me."

"You are a man after my own heart," Pulaski exclaimed.

"I know who you are!" Bentalou cried. "You are the famous Pole—Casimir Pulaski—please let me serve under you!"

Casimir had found his first recruit. "I'll meet you in Chester," he promised. "I am sure I can arrange the appointment."

As soon as word of his commission as brigadier general was published in Chester, Casimir tried to set up the cavalry. One of his difficulties was that the American generals could not understand why cavalry should be an independent corps. They had previously used four incomplete regiments set up by Congress as units to scout and send messages and were in the habit of demanding detachments for their own daily uses. No sooner would the members of Pulaski's corps assemble than they would be scattered again. It was never able to drill together.

Rarely were there a hundred cavalry at headquarters. With the Army still in retreat, there was no time to be wasted in idle dreams of finding and training more men. Casimir applied for a commission for Lieutenant Bentalou and had to do the best he could with the material at hand.

From Chester the Army continued to fall back slowly. It crossed the Schuylkill River above the falls and recrossed it on the ford leading to the Lancaster Road ten miles west of Philadelphia. General Washington set up headquarters in Warren's Tavern and ordered the men to rest. He was sure that after taking Philadelphia the enemy would try to end the war with one final, decisive battle. He would take this opportunity to hold a council of war and map out plans.

Every day Casimir went out scouting, with Lieutenant Bentalou by his side. Once when he was scouring the countryside with his cavalry, he found to his surprise that the whole British Army was approaching in forced march. He charged into the astonished van, and having forced it to retreat galloped at full speed back to headquarters to report to General Washington. It was then eleven in the morning. As he rushed to the door of headquarters, the young guard cried:

"Halt! You can't go in."

"I must see the commander at once," Pulaski protested.

"General Washington is holding a council of war. Orders—no one can enter," the guard insisted.

"Step back," Casimir shouted, frantic that even a moment was being lost. General Washington, hearing the scuffle in the next room, opened the door. He was followed by his aide, Colonel Hamilton, who spoke French very well. Casimir poured out the unexpected news.

"You have made a mistake perhaps," Colonel Hamilton observed coldly. "You have seen some of our own people."

"Seen our own people!" Casimir flew into a rage. "I have just fought a skirmish with the British!"

George Washington asked Colonel Hamilton to translate what was being said. Then, turning to Pulaski, he asked him: "What do you advise?"

"Give me three hundred infantry, and with my cavalry I can hold the enemy until you are ready," was the prompt reply.

General Washington called to Brigadier General Scott to follow Casimir, and ordered the Army to take battle positions. Tents, cook pans, bedrolls were thrown pell-mell into the carts, which were sent off down the road. The drums rumbled "to arms, to arms!" and the men fanned out behind the stone walls set around the fields. Pulaski gave the order to charge. Everyone heard General Scott's men firing across the fords.

Far from catching the American Army unaware, the British themselves drew back. They would have been routed had not the heavens given them unexpected help. A sudden deluge of rain like a waterfall poured down so hard it threw up a curtain of spray. The powder on both sides could not be lit. Within a half hour the fields looked like lakes and the Schuylkill creek became a raging torrent. The British sounded the bugle for retreat and Casimir withdrew his cavalry while it was still possible to recross the ford.

By the time the American lines had re-formed on the Lancaster Road, there was mud to the soldiers' knees. It was midnight when they reached Yellow Springs, a short distance away. They had not caught up with their baggage, but because of the heavy mud they could go no farther. Far from letting up, it was raining harder. Wood was so wet the men could not build fires for supper. The hungry soldiers improvised tents from their blankets and lay down on branches stacked on the boggy ground.

Next morning it was still drizzling. The men found their muskets so rusty that even had they had the powder handy, they could not have fired their guns. But the enemy, separated by five miles of heavy mud, could not have gone into battle either since their arms, too, were out of order. They retired to Germantown.

This gave Washington the chance to lay careful and detailed plans to surprise the British. Pulaski and his cavalry were to open the charge. The infantry were to follow close behind.

The next three nights were spent bringing up the troops in the darkness to a position near Germantown. Low-lying clouds, an aftermath of the storm, cut off the light of the moon and the stars. The soggy earth deadened every footstep. The Americans stole up to the British lines before dawn. Muffled orders were given and the horses' hoofs were padded in cloth. Pulaski, followed by his cavalry, sped forward at a gallop and captured the British outposts before they had time to give the alarm. The sleeping army simply tumbled to its feet and ran away leaving much of its valuable equipment behind.

For the second time, just as General Washington believed he had won a great victory, fate and the weather turned against him. A thick blanket of fog smothered the battlefield. The dense mist that concealed the enemy made it impossible for him to force the British to surrender. The Americans found themselves shooting their own companions. Various units lost touch with each other and dared not overwhelm Germantown, as they had planned, for fear of shooting their own men. Platoon commanders hesitated, waiting for the fog to lift. In the meantime the enemy rallied and the victory was lost.

This was a terrible blow to Casimir. Had his men been armed with lances, they could have pursued the British out of town into open country. Hand-to-hand street fighting could have been avoided where there was the danger of American troops firing into each other. After the Battle of Germantown, he had a lance made and sent it to Congress begging permission to use lances in his corps. He was refused. Neither the general staff nor Congress understood this European weapon any more than they understood the use of a true cavalry corps capable of carrying out independent missions. For them cavalry was just a part of the infantry. Casimir was to suffer many heartbreaking moments before the American Army finally adopted his ideas.

All through the winter of 1778, Congress wasted its time in endless discussions and futile recriminations. It blamed Washington for the disaster at Brandywine and for not winning a decisive victory at Germantown as General Gates had won at Saratoga. There were cries of: "Demote him and give General Gates the command."

These interminable debates sounded all too familiar to Casimir. He had always felt that the politicians were in a large measure responsible for the defeat and downfall of his beloved Poland. They sounded equally sinister here. He saw the same lack of loyalty to the soldiers who had bravely risked their lives for their country. His own experience with Congress had shown him how the needs of the army of General Washington were neglected. The men were unpaid. They needed uniforms, munitions, everything.

All his sympathy went out to the valiant commander now being slandered by so many members of Congress. When General Gates, the smooth politician, was given a place on the Board of War it became clear that General Washington would have still further difficulties.

Pulaski determined to help Washington with all his strength, using his cavalry to hit the enemy as hard as possible. He was everywhere at once. Though the raids were on a small scale, they showed his ingenuity. At the Battle of Chestnut Hill, where the American ranks had been broken, his little cavalry corps arrived in the nick of time and turned a disaster into victory. British detachments tried to avoid meeting him when they went out foraging for provisions. They well knew if Pulaski found them they would return to camp empty-handed.

After this Casimir again wrote a memorandum to General Washington to stress the American need of more cavalry. "When we are superior in cavalry, the enemy will not dare to extend theirs. We will then have many opportunities of attacking and destroying him by degrees. But if they have it in their power to augment their cavalry, they can do the same to us and ours will suffer and dwindle away. Our army dispersed and pursued by their horsemen will be unable to rally. Our baggage can be captured, our officers taken, our losses fatal."

General Washington, however, was too distraught with his own immediate problems to go to Congress and demand the means of supplying Pulaski. His own supreme command was in debate.

8

Winter of Disappointment

WHEN THE AMERICAN GENERALS decided to retire to winter quarters at Valley Forge instead of waging an all-out campaign to recover Philadelphia, Pulaski was in despair. He had voted against this decision because his most successful battles in Poland had been fought in winter and he knew the advantages of this kind of warfare. He begged Washington to reconsider, but the commander in chief would not move against the decision of the majority of his generals. He ordered Pulaski and his cavalry into winter quarters, at first in Valley Forge, then, when it became clear the horses could not be protected in the snow and bitter cold, to Trenton. There, during the long winter, Pulaski tried to drill a fighting corps out of the four very disunified cavalry regiments under his command. This presented many problems as the regimental commanders were jealous of his position.

Colonel Stephen Moylan caused him the greatest difficulties. As senior officer of the American cavalry he had expected to be given the over-all command at the time Pulaski was made brigadier general. Moylan constantly made fun of Pulaski's poor English and would often mimic Casimir to the great merriment of the junior officers. What Moylan lacked in experience he made up for in self-confidence. He loudly complained of Pulaski's orders and deemed as "fancy tricks" the feats of horsemanship Pulaski was trying to teach his men.

Moylan brought about a crisis when John Zelinski, Casimir's cousin and a former Knight of the Holy Cross, arrived in Trenton. He was one of a number of Polish Knights and French officers who, when they heard Pulaski was in charge of the American cavalry, had come to America to join their beloved leader. Moylan did not like "foreigners" and would often make remarks which they regarded as insulting. One day, as Casimir and his cousin, acting as his aide, were inspecting the corps, a dispute arose and Moylan hit Zelinski and swore at Pulaski.

Casimir instantly charged Moylan with "cowardly ungentlemanly action in striking Lieutenant Zelinski," and ordered his arrest. A court-martial was called for a few days later, but most of the American officers also resented the foreigners and Moylan was acquitted. Casimir then appealed to General Washington, but he upheld the verdict of the court. This was a severe blow to the Polish general who was offering his life to his new country and asked nothing but loyalty in return.

As soon as Moylan was freed from arrest, Lieutenant Zelinski challenged him to a duel. Moylan refused to fight "a bloody foreigner" and swore to horsewhip the young man. The next time the two met, Moylan drew his sword but the Polish Knight was more skillful and unseated him with his lance. The trick was so neatly turned that Moylan found himself standing on the ground, his horse away at a canter, before he knew what had happened. Although he did not carry out his threat to bring charges against Zelinski, he continued to make life difficult for Pulaski.

On the other hand, Colonel Theodoric Bland, commander of the Virginia regiment, quickly realized that Pulaski had the experience needed as commander in chief of the American cavalry. He himself

had received his only training in the Virginia Militia and was eager to learn modern techniques. The two came from old-fashioned homes very much alike. Neither of the men was being paid for his military services. Each was fighting for principles that he felt bound to serve as a point of honor. Both loved daring and courage. They understood each other in spite of language difficulties, and a mutual respect grew into a truer friendship with the passing of each day.

"Here," Casimir said, "it is just as it was back home, though fortunately the British are less active than the Russians. How can Congress expect anything brilliant when fifty of my men have to face a thousand better-mounted British? Remember last week when we nearly took those regiments of infantry?"

"With a second platoon we would have forced them to surrender," Bland agreed. "Even so Lord Howe doesn't dare send out less than two thousand men and two hundred horses."

"God and the geographic position of America are all that keep the British from success," Casimir remarked. "There were differences of opinion in Poland, but had we had half the advantages the Americans enjoy, we could have defeated half the European powers."

"Come now," Bland replied, "you forget how we keep the enemy hopping. Scarcely a day goes by without a skirmish."

"When they run away we fight to get their equipment," Casimir agreed. "That is why I tell you the situation reminds me of Poland. Ammunition is what we seize from the British, not what we get from Congress."

In addition to his trouble with Colonel Moylan, Casimir was constantly harassed by lack of provisions. The merchants and Tory farmers took advantage of the high prices the British were paying, and refused to supply the American Army. There was not a load of hay in Trenton. Casimir wrote

Washington: "With the greatest difficulty we have managed to put our heads under cover. To keep the horses alive I have dispersed them two miles out of town." Casimir then decided to act on the assumption that since the Tories were helping the British they were enemies and should be treated as such. So when he needed horses he sent out parties to commandeer them in New Jersey or Pennsylvania. When food was lacking, they also seized hay and corn, paying for them in Continental dollars.

The farmers appealed to Congress, and even though they were Tories, General Washington ordered Pulaski to desist. Pulaski then begged the citizens of Trenton to support his men and their horses with food, and in return he promised to defend them. But all in vain. He had to divide his beloved corps. He sent Moylan and the regiment under Baylor to Flemington and Colonel Bland to Pennytown. Thus the winter dragged by, interrupted every day by petty annoyances which interfered with the training of the cavalry corps.

Meanwhile, General Washington was forced to a desperate move. Congress paid no more attention to his appeals for supplies than they had paid to Pulaski. The suffering of his men became intense. They lacked the barest essentials of food and clothing. Because Washington could not let them starve to death, he sent out General Anthony Wayne to scour southern New Jersey for five thousand head of cattle to be bought from the farmers.

General Wayne crossed the Delaware at Wilmington. As he marched through Jersey the farmers laughed at him. They weren't going to sell their good cattle for that worthless Continental currency! All Wayne was able to buy were a few half-starved cows that were only skin and bones. But worse was to follow.

When Lord Howe heard of this expedition, he sent out three thousand troops from Philadelphia, under the command of Colonel Stirling, to capture the American party and the cattle they had collected. General Wayne learned that the British were on the move and although he was ignorant of their purpose, he felt the need of cavalry to scout their position. So he sent posthaste for Pulaski. His rider appeared just as Casimir and Colonel Bland, who had ridden over from Pennytown, were deep in plans for their coming cavalry training maneuvers.

"What is this?" Casimir exclaimed as he opened Wayne's letter. A frown gathered on his brow as he read it. In the past he had been indignant over the constant dispersal of troops he was trying to whip into shape as a really useful part of the Army. This was the last straw! He felt he would never be able to train his men properly.

"Listen," he exploded, "General Wayne is demanding a detachment of cavalry at once at Haddonsfield. This means we must again delay our maneuvers. And why does he send for me? He knows I am responsible only to General Washington as Commander in Chief."

Pulaski then tossed the letter to Colonel Bland who read it over. "It is certainly strange you have not received word from General Washington," he agreed. "Only the Commander in Chief can give orders."

"I suppose if I have to leave, it had better be at once," said Casimir. And he shouted for Bentalou to join him.

"May I go with you?" Bland asked. "I can have my men ready and here in an hour."

"Thanks," Casimir said, smiling. "I'll be glad for your help."

The camp was instantly in a fever of preparation as two hundred and fifty men saddled their horses. They set off that very evening and reached Burlington where the fatigue of men and horses forced them to rest for the few hours that remained until dawn.

Casimir's indignation had mounted with each hour since the coming of Wayne's letter. That night he sat down and wrote out his resignation to General Washington. He stated, however, that he was on his way to Wayne's relief and would give him whatever support he needed. Even as he was writing, a messenger sent by General Washington was vainly seeking Pulaski in Trenton. The letter he carried informed Pulaski of Wayne's dangerous position and asked for his help. Had he known of this Casimir would not have dispatched his letter of resignation.

The following day, in a raging snowstorm, Pulaski and Bland, still ignorant of the reason for Wayne's summons, plowed with their men along the road to Haddonsfield. When they reached General Wayne's encampment, Casimir gave voice to his exasperation. "Why," he demanded of Wayne, "does my cavalry have to be torn apart every time you set off on a little expedition?"

"What!" General Wayne exclaimed. "Had you no orders from the Commander in Chief! The courier must have been captured. The enemy surrounds us on all sides."

"Do you mean they are already in the neighborhood?" Casimir demanded. "If so, the time to strike is now."

Though his men and horses were fatigued from traveling through heavy snow, Casimir realized that they must attack at once to take advantage of the howling blizzard. As night fell, his cavalry would be invisible. The British, taken by surprise, would be unable to see how few they were in number.

It was just as Casimir had predicted. The English were amazed when he charged their outposts, and he took many prisoners on the first attack. The others broke and fled, reporting that Wayne had received large numbers of reinforcements.

Under cover of darkness the British Colonel Stirling withdrew all his troops. By dawn he was on the bank of the Delaware River preparing to retreat to Philadelphia.

Generals Pulaski and Wayne followed close behind. They pursued the British to a point where they could watch every move of the enemy. Casimir wanted to charge at once. General Wayne said they would lose their advantage if the English could see how few cavalry there really were. He persuaded

Casimir to wait for the infantry to come up. Despite much arguing between them the discussion was impersonal. Both were entirely devoted to the American cause. Pulaski and Wayne were always ready for a battle and among the most loyal officers under Washington's command. They could quarrel vehemently yet remain good friends because the American cause held the first place in their hearts.

At last the weary infantry of General Wayne arrived and was stationed on either flank of the cavalry. Together they charged into the British forces. Colonel Stirling called for the guns on English ships to open fire. The Americans withdrew, pursued by the British. As soon as they were out of range of the ship's guns, the cavalry charged again. As usual in battle Casimir was all over the field at once inspiring the men to greater enthusiasm and courage. When his horse was shot out from under him, he jumped on another. All afternoon the battle moved back and forth, the Americans trying to lure Colonel Stirling out of range of his guns.

As darkness fell once more, Colonel Stirling was forced to abandon all his supplies and ferried what was left of his men across the Delaware. Both American generals at once reported the victory to General Washington. Casimir wrote of General

Wayne: "He knows he has abused his authority, and that as commander of the cavalry, I follow no orders than those of my Commander in Chief. But my zeal for your service surpassed this point of honor. I agreed to do everything he found advantageous and acted accordingly. As a general I cannot complain of anything."

In his report General Wayne praised Pulaski. "He behaved with his usual courage and bravery and put his cavalry to good use. Without him this victory would not have been possible."

When General Washington received Pulaski's resignation he was disappointed but understood something of the motives that caused it. In his acceptance he wrote: "Your intention to resign is founded on reasons which I presume make you think it necessary. I can only say that it will always give me pleasure to hear testimony to the zeal and bravery you have displayed on every occasion."

As soon as General Washington was certain Pulaski was resigning the post of brigadier general of cavalry, Stephen Moylan was ordered to Trenton. When the news came, Moylan was overjoyed. He congratulated himself that "the foreigner's goose was cooked." He took up his headquarters, confident that the position of brigadier general would any day be his, since the other colonels had been told to obey his orders.

But he was destined to disappointment. Washington decided against a separate cavalry corps. Throughout the entire Revolutionary War Moylan kept the position of senior colonel. The four regiments remained as before, disunited units of militia, limited as to duty and usefulness.

9

Pulaski's Legion

IN SPITE OF HIS RESIGNATION as brigadier general of cavalry, Pulaski was still determined to fight for the American cause. On March 15, 1778, he went to Valley Forge to lay before the Commander in Chief a new plan for forming an independent mobile legion, composed of both cavalry and infantry. It would be placed immediately under Washington's command to be used as a spearhead in any campaign.

Pulaski found Washington at his wit's end. Many of his men had gone home sick from the terrible cold of the winter, the lack of food and inadequate clothing. He was interested in Pulaski's plan but told him he was having difficulty filling his own ranks with new recruits. He advised Casimir to ask

Congress for a very small unit, since it was in no mood to spend money.

Casimir at once drew up a petition to Congress. His specifications for the legion were modest: he suggested three companies of lancers supported by three companies of infantry. They would be trained like the ancient Roman legions to work closely together. He begged for quick action so that the new legion could be prepared for the coming campaign.

At the same time General Washington wrote to Mr. Laurens, president of the Congress, saying he wished to back the proposal of Pulaski. He offered suggestions regarding the recruiting of this independent legion, saying he thought Pulaski should find the cavalrymen among Americans who could pay for their own horses and who could receive the Continental reward for prisoners as their pay. The infantry could be taken from the draft unless its ranks could be filled by volunteers. Washington ended his letter by pointing out that the "valor and disinterested zeal he [Pulaski] has shown do him great honor, and he is entitled to retain his rank as brigadier general."

When Congress asked the Board of War to advise them about the new legion, Pulaski received unexpected support. General Charles Lee, who earlier in his career had fought with the Russians against Poland and knew Pulaski's reputation, wrote: "I sincerely hope Congress will double the number of his troops, as I am persuaded his principle of maneuvering is admirable and will render essential service to our country. He should have at least eight hundred men and twelve hundred horse lancers." Four days later the Board of War approved the Legion and recommended a much more powerful force than Casimir had himself timidly suggested.

Two weeks after Casimir had resigned from the regular cavalry, Congress approved his independent Legion. But they did not follow the recommendation of General Charles Lee and the Board of War; instead, they authorized sixty-eight horsemen and two hundred infantry to be raised as General Washington thought best. Though it was the smallest unit Casimir had ever commanded, he wasted no time lobbying for a larger force but joyfully set up his new command in Baltimore. Even with such a modest group he would make himself useful to the American cause.

General Washington gave Pulaski permission to choose his own officers from among the four existing cavalry regiments; he was to take a few from each in order to have a small nucleus of trained men. Many from these regiments wished to volunteer, but except for Major Bedkin, who had resigned in disgust from Colonel Moylan's regiment at the time of the affair of Zelinski, Casimir chose only those who had followed him from Europe or joined him after he became brigadier general. Among these were his cousin Lieutenant Zelinski and other former Knights of the Holy Cross. These he made captains. Major Bedkin became paymaster of the Legion and the young French officer Paul Bentalou, who had never left Pulaski's side, became his aide and adjutant.

Casimir settled in Baltimore, Maryland, where he and his men would have adequate facilities for the practice of their Catholic religion during the time they were preparing for their service. After he had established headquarters in a house in Baltimore, he sent out his officers to find recruits. They set up stations in Maryland, Virginia, Pennsylvania and New Jersey where the name of the Polish cavalry commander was already well known. In every town where recruiting offices were opened the newspapers carried the following announcement:

"All who desire to distinguish themselves in the service of their country are invited to enlist in the Legion. Opportunity will be offered to enterprising, brave, vigilant soldiers. They will prefer the Legion to other services not destined to harass the enemy so much. As time for action is approaching, those desiring to distinguish themselves should apply immediately."

In Baltimore, Casimir made preparations to equip his new volunteers. He galloped from saddlemaker to saddlemaker, testing the leather of the one against that of the other. Only the finest quality of everything would suit his exacting demands. Congress had granted him $150 to outfit each man. He oversaw the making of the three pairs of shoes each was to receive with the same care as though they were to be his own. The cavalrymen were to have lances; for these he chose wood that would bend without snapping, and he put a mark on each piece as it was tested. He even ordered the underdrawers, shirts and stockings himself. The ironmongers with whom he dealt trembled for fear lest he find fault with the lance tips or with the bits, bridles and currycombs for the horses. There were carbines, cartridge boxes, and saddlebags to be issued each man, and finally the caps and cloaks. These uniforms were designed to protect the soldiers in all kinds of weather; they were in sky-blue cloth with scarlet, green, white, yellow or orange wool linings. He even tested the linen for the pockets and the strength of the thread to be used. He ordered five thousand handkerchiefs and ten thousand gold metal buttons to trim the uniforms.

People asked, "Why do you need uniforms in so many colors?"

"So I can tell at a glance," Casimir replied, "to which company each man belongs. When I need to change their positions I can do it more quickly."

By June 10 the supplies began to roll in, and none too soon. Casimir already had a hundred more volunteers than Congress had authorized. Men flocked to serve under such a famous commander. When some other generals protested that their men were leaving to join the Legion, these men were sent back. The ranks of the Legion were closed when three hundred and sixty men had been obtained. Casimir had personally interviewed most of the recruits. Each man had to show special qualifications.

He was far more exacting in training his men than any other officer under whom they had previously served. During the humid, exhausting heat of early summer, the men were drilled day after day. For three months the cavalry were taught stunts on horseback until the horse and rider seemed one. Sword in one hand and lance in the other, they galloped zigzag across the field, slashing at posts set up as dummies. Then, rearing their steeds, they would wheel about-face in an instant to charge in the opposite direction.

Although Congress had appropriated $50,000 to outfit the Legion, it was slow in paying out the money. Pulaski wrote his sister Anna, the nun, still living in her convent near Warsaw, directing her to sell one of the family farms. She sent him $16,000 which he quickly spent on the needs of the Legion. As the shoemakers completed each pair of boots for his men, to save time Pulaski would pay for them out of his own pocket. When items were small, he did not bother to get receipts. He had always disliked filling out forms and keeping accounts. Now time seemed all too short to get his men in the field, and every interruption by bookkeepers asking him to sign vouchers seemed to him an unnecessary delay.

Nearly every day Pulaski rode down to the port. Many of his supplies came by ship and most of the outfitters had warehouses on the water fronts. One morning he noticed a brig for sale. At once he sat down and wrote the governor of Maryland asking for the use of the ship. "My soldiers," he wrote, "must be instructed in the marine and be like the Roman troops who could serve anywhere on land and sea." He foresaw the day when the British would leave and when a marine corps would be useful, with its own infantry, cavalry and artillery.

The boat in question was involved in a lawsuit, and the Council of Maryland could not advise its use. Although they were not in a position to help Pulaski start the marine corps, which has become such a great tradition in our history, they replied: "General Pulaski's defense of the liberties of mankind in general, and his especial attachment to the liberties of America, entitle him to our attentive regard."

For the moment Casimir had to give up his idea of a marine corps. Besides, he was more than ever anxious to get his men in the field. When he heard of General Charles Lee's defeat at the Battle of Monmouth, Casimir could not help being disappointed that his Legion had not been called into action. In his heart he believed they might have turned the defeat into victory.

He spent the month of July giving his forces their final polish, sparing no time for his personal pleasures and for the summer balls or dinner parties to which he was invited. The beautiful girls in their fluttering organdies and ribbons, sitting beside their mothers as they watched the drill from their carriages on the edge of the parade grounds, held no place in his life. He nodded to them gravely as he galloped by, but his eyes were on his men.

On August 4 the *Maryland Journal* noted: "General Pulaski reviewed his independent legion in this town. Their martial appearance excited the admiration of all. They performed many maneuvers in a manner that reflected the highest honor on both officers and privates."

Casimir wished he could hear such praise from the lips of Congress itself, for he needed its permission to be given an assignment. He should have sent to Philadelphia vouchers for the money he had spent, and he knew that he had trained more men than Congress had agreed upon. Instead of attending to these matters he marched his troops north for a gala parade into Philadelphia. Casimir Pulaski had never known how to deal with politicians.

The men marched under a beautiful red satin banner embroidered by the Moravian sisters at Bethlehem, Pennsylvania. He had carefully chosen the emblem, one acceptable to both Protestants and Catholics. On one side "U.S." was circled with the words *Unita Virtus Fortior* (Union Makes for Valor). On the other was a picture of the all-seeing Eye of God surrounded by thirteen stars representing the thirteen states and the words *Non Alius Regit* (None Other Rules).

The glittering parade of the Legion into Philadelphia was watched by the citizens with great excitement. No one had seen anything like it; even the British troops with their red coats and white trousers could not rival the legionnaires. Each dragoon was mounted on his own fine horse; his sky-blue cloak was thrown back to display the bright linings. Each had a cap to match, cocked to the right, with gold metal buttons shining in the sun.

"Hurrah for the Legion," the people shouted. "Hurrah, hurrah," echoed through the town. Although the Tories scoffed that the Legion was so small, the patriots, who had hung their heads in shame during the British occupation, stamped and shouted with pride. Nothing could dampen their spirits.

With a fanfare of bugles the procession reached the steps of the courthouse where the members of Congress stood waiting as the men marched by. Each company saluted smartly to the rattle of drums.

Although the members of Congress had joined in cheering his men, when Casimir asked permission to go into immediate action, it hesitated. First it wanted Pulaski to settle all his accounts. Since he had paid for his equipment in American money rather than in English pounds, some shopkeepers were appealing to Congress for his arrest. General Washington, too, had paid in the same way, and later on Congress was forced to make a ruling to protect its money or lose all its authority. But now Pulaski was kept waiting for these matters to be settled when there was so much he could have accomplished in the field.

After two weeks of waiting, Casimir wrote Congress: "I blush to find myself still languishing in a state of inactivity. The review is passed, there remains for me but to ask for the payment of my soldiers, the commission of the officers and permission to march against the enemy. This is what I take the liberty to request."

Fortunately for Pulaski, on September 19 he received direct orders from General Washington:

"As soon as the Board gives the Legion the order to move, they are to join my Army east of New York City, at Kingsbridge on the North River." He added in postscript: "If, as you pass through Jersey, the enemy has landed in that state, give General Maxwell every assistance you can with your corps."

10

Treachery at Little Egg Harbor

THE MESSAGE from General Washington stirred Congress and the Board of War to action. A command was issued for the Legion to march. At last the months of preparation would be put to the test, and Casimir joyfully set off at once. The crowds which had welcomed the Legion into Philadelphia again lined the streets to wave them good-bye. This time there was no parade; the men marched beside their creaking baggage wagons as they jolted over the cobblestones, piled high with bedding and tents, mess-kits and extra ammunition.

The columns wound out of the city along the old Trenton road. The men were laying bets as to whether they would meet the British before they reached New York when suddenly a rider on horseback, hoofs flying, came thundering toward them.

"Who goes there?" he was challenged by the van.

"A message to General Pulaski from the Commander in Chief," the rider replied.

Casimir, as was his habit, was riding up and down the column to chat with his captains and to look over his men, for whose needs he was ever alert. News of the messenger from General Washington passed down the column faster than the rider himself could gallop. When it reached Casimir, he raced back to the head of the line. There he learned that General Washington had ordered the Legion to proceed at once to the Jersey shore. The men threw their caps in the air and cheered when they heard the change of orders.

In his letter General Washington explained that Lord Howe had just sent a British fleet manned by seven hundred Tories to Barnegat Bay to capture the fleet of small American vessels operating out of Little Egg Harbor and successfully running the blockade established by the British Navy at the mouth of the Delaware River. This new British move was to stop them. If they did so, the enemy would gain control of the entire coast.

While Pulaski was on his forced march across the Jersey flats, the British landed without opposition at Little Egg Harbor. Fortunately when their ships were sighted most of the American boats had been dragged up Little Egg and Mullica creeks, both too shallow for the larger British transatlantic vessels to enter. But while the Americans were saving their boats, the British proceeded to burn down all the houses in the two villages of Chestnut Neck and Bay's River Neck as well as the sawmill needed to keep the local boats in repair.

Pulaski's Legion reached the shore on October 6, while the houses were still smoldering. They had been joined by artillery corps under Colonel Proctor and the local Jersey and Pennsylvania militia. On seeing the American Army the Tories under British command scrambled back into their boats in the harbor and trained their guns on shore. Casimir set up his camp within sight of the anchored enemy vessels but outside their range. He then called for a meeting between Colonel Proctor and the militia commanders to draw up plans for stationing their troops.

The first troop of light dragoons was placed in the center facing the harbor. To their right was a picket of fifty infantry under the Legion's Colonel de Botzen, to the left a part of the Jersey militia. The main body of infantry was placed behind, well hidden in a thick wood. The entrance to the harbor was guarded by Proctor's artillery on one side and the Jersey militia on the other; these were alerted to stand by on either shore of the bay to prevent the British from escaping through the inlet out to sea.

De Botzen had come from Germany to join the American Army because he had no sympathy for the Prussian autocratic spirit of Frederick the Great. He had later transferred to Pulaski's Legion. Among his men were three former Hessian officers who had deserted to the American side during the previous winter. Congress had suggested that Pulaski take them into his Legion without giving them commissions, although one of them, Gustav Juliet, had the duties of sublieutenant.

Colonel de Botzen held Juliet and his companions in contempt as deserters. "How," he would ask them, "can commissioned officers forsake their colors?" He disliked them heartily, did not trust them, and wished they would learn enough English to be moved into one of the other companies.

Soon after the pickets under Colonel de Botzen were settled in their quarters, Juliet asked permission to go fishing, saying he had heard that snappers were running in Mullica Creek, that he and his companion would soon be back with enough fish to feed the whole picket. When this happened Pulaski was out scouting and De Botzen granted Juliet and his companions three hours' leave, since no action was expected until the artillery could set up its guns.

The Hessians did not return at the end of the time and De Botzen sent out men to look for them. When last seen Juliet and his two friends had been embarking in a dory and had disappeared from view into Barnegat Bay. Although a heavy sea was piling up, a boat was sent out into the bay to look for them. When the searching party returned to Colonel de Botzen, it reported that no sign of Juliet and his companions could be found. It was supposed they must have drowned as only experienced boatmen could handle a dory in such weather.

Colonel de Botzen's first thought was "good riddance." Had they been any other of his men, he would have reported at once to Pulaski, but in this instance he thought he would wait until morning. The picket settled down for the night. Guards were posted outside the house serving as headquarters and De Botzen undressed and went to bed. Three days of forced march had been exhausting. He quickly fell asleep.

In the meantime treachery was afoot. Juliet and his companions rowed out to the British flagship *Zebra* and offered to guide the enemy to Pulaski's headquarters. Juliet used the name "Brownville" so the British would not know he was one of the deserters for whom they had published a reward.

As soon as it was dark, the British slipped two hundred and fifty men into rowboats and glided stealthily to shore. The pounding of the waves along the shore and the croaking of the frogs in the creek rose above every sound. They concealed their rowboats among the rustling reeds and left fifty men to guard them. The rest crept silently through the woods and surrounded De Botzen's quarters without his guards hearing a sound. The signal to charge waked De Botzen who, pistol in hand, ran downstairs in his nightshirt.

As he opened the door, Juliet cried, "That's the one, that is your man, kill him!" De Botzen fought like a lion but he was overpowered by numbers and killed with bayonets. Pulaski's close friend, Lieutenant de la Borderie, and about twenty-five of the pickets in that outpost were also butchered. Thus Juliet was avenged.

At the crack of the first pistol Pulaski, who never seemed to sleep, was on horseback with his cavalry

galloping after him. They arrived too late to save De Botzen, but they prevented the British from burning down the house where the rest of the pickets were still firing from the windows. Some of the enemy scattered into the woods; others on the way to their boats tore up the bridge that crossed the creek. But Pulaski took forty prisoners and captured all the ammunition the British and Tories brought ashore.

Before the remnant of the enemy landing party could return to their ships, Pulaski ordered his artillery to open fire. The British tried to save the flagship *Zebra*, which went aground. Twenty of the British prize ships were also burned. The rest of the fleet escaped to sea. The entire enemy losses could not be estimated, and the British and Tories had suffered a smashing defeat. The damage to the Americans was slight in comparison, but Casimir mourned the loss of two of his most trusted officers. This bitterness took all the joy out of his victory.

Casimir spent the next few days rounding up the enemy survivors who had scattered in the woods. They were being hidden by neighboring Tories who absolutely refused to give them up, and there was no way of capturing these soldiers without burning down private houses. In his report to Congress, recounting the whole affair and the capture of a large stock pile of booty, Pulaski suggested that all Americans be forced to take an oath of allegiance.

"Those Tories," he grumbled to Captain Bentalou, "look on us as worse than their own enemies. They fire on us at night and send us off on the wrong road and have the impudence to complain to Congress that the British cause less damage than the troops sent to protect them."

General Washington lost no time choosing a new assignment for the Legion. All summer long he had had to refuse help to the colonists in upper New York State where the British, operating out of Fort Niagara, were raiding the settlers with the help of Indian warriors. Terrible reports of scalping parties and Governor Clinton's appeals for help had to go unanswered. Until now he had no troops to spare, but as soon as Washington learned of Pulaski's successful action on the Jersey coast, and that he was begging for another assignment, he ordered the Legion to Minisink, New York.

"Governor Clinton," he wrote Pulaski on November 10, "advises Minisink on the Delaware River. There will be plenty of fodder there for the horses. It is near Cole's Fort, which should be strengthened. Let your cavalry and infantry be quartered as near as possible in case the Indians attack the inhabitants."

Casimir jumped at the opportunity for action. He had never been in the American wilderness and, since none of his officers were experienced as backwoodsmen, this adventure would test their abilities in still another kind of warfare.

The Legion set out along the Delaware River which wound through high, rugged mountains. Soon the road narrowed to a trail, and the column stretched back more than a mile. There were frequent stops to repair the log road or to shovel aside rubble that had fallen from overhanging crags. Without his experience in the Polish mountains, Casimir would never have been able to lead his cavalry up to Minisink.

As they pushed deeper into the wilderness, Casimir came to know the difficulties of leading cavalry through the forest. Quantities of oats had to be carried for the horses, and their feet became sore from the rough trails. Frequent stops had to be made to set up forges for the blacksmiths to fashion new horseshoes. At the Delaware Water Gap the trail led over the mountains and the wagons had to be pushed and tugged up the steep, narrow trail. The scouts kept a constant lookout for Indians, and each company had to forage for game to replenish its stock of fresh food.

Winter was closing in. Casimir worried about their slow progress, for they must reach Minisink before heavy snow made traveling impossible. He was alarmed, too, by the reports of terrible Indian and Tory raids. The Tories were said to be more savage than the Indians. They had burned farmhouses and carried off families from whom no word was ever heard again. Those who were not killed otherwise were scalped.

When they arrived they found Cole's Fort no longer standing. It had been burned during the summer! Overcoming his dismay, Casimir quickly set up headquarters across the river in the village of Rosecrantz. Local supplies of hay and forage had been burned during the raid on Cole's Fort, and it was quite clear that the cavalry horses would quickly consume what little the neighboring farmers could spare.

Casimir decided to build a new fort and wrote General Washington asking for cannon. In the same letter he asked permission to send his cavalry to a place where more food could be found. To Congress he wrote November 26, "I desired to be employed near the enemy's line. I find myself placed in a wilderness where there are only bears to fight." While waiting for replies to these two letters, quarters had to be found for the men. The soldiers chopped down trees and built log barracks which they surrounded with a strong stockade.

One dark, snowy day a stranger rode into camp. He proved to be one of the former Polish Knights, Colonel Kotkowski. Benjamin Franklin had written General Washington that he was coming almost a year before, and now he suddenly appeared to join his old friend Pulaski in Minisink. This joyful reunion was the only celebration to break Pulaski's monotonous days of chopping trees and building camp.

In the middle of December Washington wrote ordering Pulaski to leave his infantry in Minisink and to take his cavalry back to Easton, Pennsylvania on the Delaware, where he hoped they would find enough food. The next two months Casimir spent on horseback traveling between the far-separated points of Easton, Minisink and Congress in Philadelphia. Old accounts were still unsettled, and new ones were piling up. Then supplies ran out in Easton, and Washington ordered the horses sent farther south.

This meant the Legion would be still further separated. Casimir was seized with despair. What would become of his Legion, and when would he be free to go where he was most needed to fight the British? He knew the British had invaded Georgia, and here he was wasting his time struggling to settle his accounts with Congress and unable to provide food for his men. True the presence of his infantry in Minisink kept the enemy away, but that did not seem to him an active fight for freedom.

One cannot help wondering why Casimir did not resign. Yet he was loyal to his oath to fight until the British were driven from the American continent. Since he had offered his services to the Americans, he would never give up.

In February Congress, which for three months had idled over the allotment of funds for the

American Army, was forced to take action. Savannah had fallen in December and the citizens of Charleston were demanding protection for their city, which was on the line of the British march northward. All the Carolina and Virginia troops were in New York serving General Washington, and the local militia was obviously incapable of preventing the British from occupying the whole south.

Washington knew Pulaski's infantry was useless at Minisink as far as active fighting was concerned and on February 2 he ordered them south. Casimir was delighted at this order. For the first time since his Legion was organized it would be the spearhead of an entire campaign! He was filled with enthusiasm at the prospect. Before leaving for the south, however, he made another attempt to have Congress raise his corps to regimental size.

Though Congress at first refused, on February 15 it yielded. It was clear that the Legion had sufficient officers to lead far more men. Congress finally appropriated the $50,000 to pay those already in the corps, but not the new recruits they had authorized to be picked up along the way. Then it delayed making even this sum available.

Yet Casimir went ahead with his preparations and set up his headquarters in Lancaster to await the arrival of the infantry from Minisink. Every day small detachments arrived. They reported that the inhabitants there, who had been so unfriendly in the beginning, were now trying to prevent their leaving, and that they were sending protests to Congress against the removal of the Legion. Farmers who had previously refused to sell them food had pleaded with the troops to stay, and indeed their fears were justified. The moment the Legion left Minisink, the British and Indians swooped down on the people and massacred them.

When Pulaski's entire Legion had assembled in Lancaster, the march south was laid out. Gentlemen from the Carolinas and Virginia gave advice on the best roads for the Army to travel and sent their own men ahead to prepare for the reception of the Legion in the various towns along the way. He was ready to leave, but Congress still dallied.

11

Victory at Charleston

TIME WAS RUNNING OUT. Fearing that Charleston would fall before Congress would authorize the sums he needed, Casimir decided to start his Legion out while he himself would wait a little while longer.

He decided to send the infantry first. It was to march down through the Shenandoah Valley, where the roads were better for the baggage wagons, the countryside was richer, and there more doctors and medicines could be found for the soldiers who became sick. There was the added advantage that this route passed through the finest farm lands of the South where food for the men and horses was easily available. A second detachment—a troop of dragoons and a picked company of light infantry under

Captain Bentalou—was sent to Williamsburg, the capital of Virginia. They had instructions to find recruits and obtain supplies from the governor.

In the meantime Casimir moved his main body of cavalry to York. He waited in Pennsylvania ten days after the departure of the infantry, and then wrote Congress a final letter before starting south:

"My march has been stopped on my arrival in this town by the absence of the quartermaster appointed to provide and pay for the forages for the Legion along the road. The infantry left here the 18th and I have sent the Board of War a copy of the orders I gave to be observed during their march.

"I will set out this day. I have sent three captains to recruit three companies. Instead of $50,000 you were to deliver to me, I have received $35,000. You can see very easily this is not sufficient to supply me for the future. I beg you, gentlemen, deliver this $15,000 to the bearer of this letter who has already advanced part of his own money. Nine hundred pounds printed on the 20th of March which has been distributed to my officers and privates has no longer any value. Please order that money to be changed by the Treasurer for them."

The cavalry set off as soon as this letter was finished. They followed the same route as the infantry had taken, through Winchester, Virginia, to Staunton, where they were to climb over the pass through the mountains.

All down the valley fruit trees in full bloom brushed the men with showers of fragrant petals. On either side of the road were wide pastures where herds of fine cattle were munching the crisp green grass. Larks flying over the meadows poured out their hearts in song, and the horses, snorting and prancing in the clean spring air, had to be reined down to the slow, steady pace needed for the long journey.

Every fifteen miles or so Casimir would halt for the day and tether the horses to build up their strength after the exhausting winter which had reduced them to skin and bones. Camp would be set up near one of those large brick homesteads surrounded with sweet-smelling boxwood. Everywhere the men were given a hearty welcome to spend the night.

Casimir could not help but think of Winiary as he went to sleep between soft linen sheets to the lullaby of workers' singing after their day was done. The whole countryside reminded him of Poland. He understood his hosts perfectly, their interest in crops and farming as well as politics. These men had nothing to gain from the war. Indeed they had everything to lose if their trade were cut off from England. But they backed the American cause as a point of honor because of their belief in liberty.

Undoubtedly his good friend, Colonel Bland of Virginia and his nephew, later known as Light-Horse Harry Lee, had given Pulaski letters of introduction which opened many doors to him. But no matter where they bivouacked for the night Casimir met men whose family training had been the same as his own. He was happier than at any time since reaching America.

As he journeyed across the Blue Ridge Mountains, smaller hills rose and fell in shallower valleys until they flattened into the Carolina plains. The road wound up and down endlessly through scrubby pinewoods where the land was scanty and poor. The first break in the monotonous up and down of the Piedmont was the ferry over the river Dan. Here Pulaski learned that the infantry had passed a week before. It had taken the infantry two days to ferry their baggage wagons, their horses and all their men, but Pulaski crossed in half the time.

April was coming to an end. By now the horses were in better trim and their pace could be increased. They took the road to Charlotte, North

Carolina, and there Casimir left the cavalry to overtake the infantry. Every minute he expected to hear the British had already reached Charleston. It was a race now who would get there first. He finally overtook the infantry at Camden, South Carolina, and while waiting for the cavalry to arrive, he inspected his troops and called for volunteers to go on ahead to Charleston. With these men he pushed on without further delay, and the cavalry caught up with them a day following as they were fording a stream. Now that they were in enemy territory their scouts were constantly on the alert. But there was still no sign of the British and it was not until they reached Charleston that they learned that on that same day the enemy had crossed the Ashley River with a large army.

When he entered Charleston, Pulaski did not wait to go into action. With his own detachment and volunteers from the local militia, he went out to destroy the enemy's advance parties. Although General Prevost had thirty-six hundred men, and Pulaski, at that time, merely three hundred, he ambushed the astonished British in a wooded swamp. Before they had a chance to draw their guns, Pulaski and his men, brandishing their sabers, had slashed the pistols from the enemy's hands.

The brilliance of this maneuver drew the Charleston militia from their hiding place to watch and cheer, thus bringing on themselves a fierce line of fire. Colonel Kowacz, Pulaski's second-in-command, was killed, but when the British staggered back to regroup its shattered forces, Casimir withdrew.

Casimir returned to Charleston to find the Assembly debating on whether to surrender. They did not wish to see their beautiful city, the fourth largest in the colonies, destroyed. In view of the overwhelming superiority of the British forces, they saw no way out of the disaster hanging over them.

When Casimir strode into the assembly hall and they invited him to speak, his confident manner lifted their courage. It was not too difficult for him to persuade the Assembly to resist. Colonel Laurens, son of the president of the Continental Congress, introduced the young brigadier general of cavalry. General Moultrie, in charge of the defense of the city, had hesitated until his arrival, afraid that the outnumbered Americans would fail. But Casimir inspired everyone. The infantry of the Legion, he said, was already entering the outskirts of the city. He reported that George Washington had sent General Benjamin Lincoln with some southern troops two weeks before. They should arrive any day. He was sure Charleston could hold out until they arrived.

It soon became apparent that the British General Prevost had suffered far greater losses than were first realized. As his scouts brought in news of American reinforcements reaching Charleston he decided to withdraw to Beaufort Island to the south. He had lost so many men and officers that he needed reinforcements and at Beaufort he could be more easily supplied by sea, out of reach of the Americans.

Pulaski had no intention of letting Prevost escape so easily. With additional cavalry detachments lent by General Lincoln, he followed the enemy all the way. The road lay through low land deeply indented with broad muddy rivers, planted in a wealth of rice paddies. Clouds of malarial mosquitoes rose out of the swamps to sting and infect the men. Soon Casimir and all his legion were sick. But although they suffered terribly from heat and fever, they did not give up the chase.

In a repetition of those brilliant maneuvers Pulaski had developed in Poland, he took many British prisoners; he used captured supplies which the British abandoned, shot and killed the rear guard, forcing Prevost to fight every step to Beaufort Island

and to suffer the loss of all but eight hundred of his men.

On his return to Charleston Pulaski received a hero's welcome. General Moultrie and General Lincoln praised his boldness and his skill. No one had ever seen so many enemy troops decimated by such trifling forces. For the first time since landing in America he was acclaimed as a great military leader. When the news of these victories was carried north, even the troops under General Washington gained new courage.

To relax in the shadows of a cool stone portico overlooking Charleston Harbor was a welcome change after nearly two years of recruiting, drilling and training troops. The torrid heat was filtered by the rustling live oaks, a mint julep cooled Casimir's recurring bouts of fever; he heard the playful chatter of well-educated friends instead of the roar of guns.

Charleston, when Casimir arrived in May, 1779, was certainly the least provincial city in all the colonies. Even though it was smaller than Philadelphia, New York or Boston, it was the most beautiful and perhaps the richest of them all, its people the most cultured. Wide streets lined with pink brick houses ran down to the sparkling blue waters of the bay.

Casimir enjoyed the theater, the symphony, and even the band concerts in the park. Each night a different play by some famous dramatist could be seen. Artists from France and Italy performed at the opera house or the concert hall. The southern planters were very charitable. They had provided the first free schools and orphanages for the poor. In their private schools Latin, French, science and mathematics were taught. Casimir found even the girls were well educated at a time when most young ladies learned only needlework and good manners, and he enjoyed talking French to them.

Because of the importance of trade with England, British influence had been unusually strong in Charleston. However, shortly after the outbreak of the war, they had told the British that "they were resolved to take up arms, having fortified their minds with the conviction that they were defending the inestimable rights of Life, Liberty, and Property." Considering that by this they lost a valuable market for their rice, cotton and tobacco, it was remarkable that there were fewer Tories there than in the North.

This patriotism won Casimir's heart. He felt truly at home; and he would have been supremely happy had not his cousin, Lieutenant Zelinski, been lying severely wounded in the hospital. Many of the Legion privates were there also and every day Casimir spent many hours cheering them by his visits.

Though Casimir was made welcome in every house in Charleston, the one in which he felt most at home was that of Colonel John Laurens. The two had first met during the Battle of Brandywine, where Colonel Laurens grew to admire the young foreigner who had rushed into battle and shown so much courage. They had later seen each other at Valley Forge, and Colonel Laurens had been the first to greet Pulaski in Charleston and had introduced him to the Assembly.

Laurens' grandfather had amassed great wealth as a merchant who bought rice in the American South and sold it in Europe. Now he owned a whole fleet of ships which Casimir loved to watch being loaded at the fine new docks. Colonel Laurens owned one of the finest houses in town surrounded by four acres of garden thought to be the handsomest in the city.

In Pulaski's honor Laurens arranged many entertaining balls to which were invited all the families in society. Casimir had learned to dance while he was the page of the Duchess of Courland. But he did not know all the new minuets, hornpipes, rigadoons, pas-pied or the new cotillion. When his friend urged him to dance, he said laughingly, "That step came into the mode while I was in prison in Marseilles; I never had a chance to learn it." But he loved exchanging jokes, and when he could not dance, he could talk until sunrise.

In spite of his exploits Congress had not settled Pulaski's accounts. Nearly four months had passed since he had arrived in Charleston, and still Congress owed his men money as well as the repayment of the sum he personally had advanced to outfit the Legion. On August 19 he wrote a last letter to Congress:

"Gentlemen, is there one act of mine, since the battle of Brandywine down to the campaign of Charleston, that has not demonstrated the most disinterested zeal for the public cause? Whence comes it I have so little credit from you, gentlemen? Since I undertook to raise my corps, which I clothed, recruited, and exercised in the space of three months, I have been and still am persecuted.

"The delay of Congress to send me against the enemy was grounded on pretense. Though at Little Egg Harbor several of my officers and men fell or were wounded, their only reward was slander. My request to settle accounts was rejected. Now those are dead who should present the accounts. The sum which seems extravagant to you is but a trifle to the States. Though not rich I can pay them myself. I have lately heard from my family they are sending 100,000 pounds hard money. Should it come safely it will be a pleasure to repay you for my Legion to the last farthing.

"Be just, gentlemen. I came to hazard all for the freedom of America and to pass the rest of my life in a country truly free; and, before settling as a citizen, to fight for liberty. The campaign is at hand, and I may still have an occasion of showing you I am a friend of the cause."

In this letter Casimir Pulaski also spoke for George Washington and the other generals in the Continental Army who had fought and suffered for America, and who, in spite of the neglect and indifference of the politicians, were carrying on the battle for freedom.

All through the summer of 1779 Pulaski had suffered greatly from malaria. Every day at noon he would be seized with such violent chills that he would have fallen from his saddle had he not taken the precaution to dismount. Then for several hours he would shake all over until it seemed as though his bones rattled in their sockets. These chills were followed by such a burning fever that his faithful aide, Captain Bentalou, sometimes feared for his commander's life. In the evening, however, the fever would pass, and he would rise exhausted to complete his work for the day.

Since most of the soldiers he had brought from the North had also caught "swamp fever," as malaria was then called, Pulaski awaited only the recovery of his wounded troops in the Charleston hospital to move his headquarters to high land about fifty miles northeast of Augusta, Georgia. But once there he could not take advantage of the quiet and rest his soldiers were given. At least once a week he rode the great distance back to Charleston where he hoped for news of the French fleet which was already on its way from the West Indies to help drive the rest of the British force out of Savannah.

Each time he returned to Charleston, lively parties were given in his honor. Much as he enjoyed them, his thoughts were far too occupied with the continuous problems of campaigning ever to relax completely with his many new and pleasant friends. Yet he had made up his mind to settle in Charleston as soon as the war was ended. One summer night as he was talking to his friend, he told Colonel Laurens that when his money arrived from Poland, and Congress had been repaid for the cost of his Legion, he intended to go into trade in Charleston.

"Never begin life in Charleston as a merchant," Laurens counseled. "Buy yourself a plantation, then when you are well established, no one will think less of you if you turn tradesman."

"But they must know me now," Casimir objected.

"True you are a hero today, but as a businessman they would despise you tomorrow," Laurens pointed out.

"Your grandfather made his money as a middleman," Pulaski exclaimed.

Laurens laughed. "We've spent years trying to forget that! But I know a place you would like."

"Tell me about it after the war," Casimir interrupted. "Just now I have too much else on my mind. What of these autumn storms I have heard so much about? Do you think that D'Estaing and the French fleet have been caught in one?"

"No," Laurens assured him. "We would have heard from our own men if there were any storms on the Atlantic. Stop worrying."

"D'Estaing is a month late," Pulaski insisted.

"He will get here, never fear. Most likely his fleet is becalmed and he is cursing the lack of wind. In the meantime, have a good time. There are still many pretty girls longing to make your acquaintance."

Casimir felt too weak from the effects of his fever to make the effort. "Another time," he begged. "You will excuse me now if I prefer this dark corner. How the nightingales remind me of home! Sometimes at night I imagine I am still at our country place at Winiary; the fiddler squeaking his bow to make his music heard over the noise of chatter and laughter, and the moon trying to outshine the light from the windows."

"Sentimentalist! I'll find you a wife yet!" Laurens exclaimed.

"After the war."

Laurens lifted the glass he held in his hand. "This winter, after the war!"

Week after week Pulaski returned to Augusta without news of the French fleet. He liked to travel by night when he was certain of being free of fever and his horse was spared the heat of the day. In the morning he would report to General McIntosh before he pushed on to his own headquarters. For the first time he, his men and horses were receiving enough food from the neighboring farmers. The Southerners accepted his I O U's to be paid after the war. When he was free from fever, he was in high spirits and whistled as he rode.

Once on returning to camp he found another old Polish friend who, having heard in Europe of the coming battle in Savannah, had crossed the ocean to join Pulaski. Congress had provided him with a horse and funds for the journey. He was a fearless fighter and Casimir welcomed this addition to his forces. Not that he lacked new recruits. He had as many as he could handle; mostly young Southerners who, like the former Knights, owned their own horses and equipment and could pay their own upkeep.

Every day the cavalry rode out on patrol. During the summer they had steadily rounded up the British and driven them all back to Savannah, with the exception of Prevost's men, isolated in Beaufort. The lightning speed of the sallies made it impossible for the British to go foraging in Georgia, and they were now dependent on their ships for supplies. As soon as the French fleet arrived and they were cut off from the sea, their surrender seemed certain. No wonder Pulaski's Legion awaited the French fleet with such impatience.

12

The Battle of Savannah

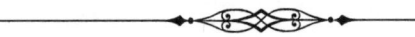

ONE DAY, soon after his return from Charleston to his camp in Augusta, as Casimir was out riding on one of his routine patrols, he met a French soldier bearing a message from Admiral d'Estaing. He learned to his joy that the French fleet had arrived off the Georgia coast. It was made up of twenty-two first-class ships, two of them carrying fifty guns, and of eight frigates. The ships carried about five thousand men. Casimir immediately sent this news to McIntosh. In reply McIntosh ordered the Legion to join his troops at once, so their combined forces could move south together. In the meantime Pulaski and he would go to Charleston to meet with the other generals for a council of war.

When the two generals reached Charleston they found its citizens in a fever of excitement at the arrival of the French chief of staff, Count de Fontanges. As Generals Lincoln, Pulaski and McIntosh rode into town to confer with the French officer, all the houses were decorated with flags and bands played in the streets. Fontanges brought word that Admiral d'Estaing was ready to land the troops in Beaulieu, Georgia, but for the Americans to hurry, as the ships carrying the French reinforcements could not long remain in those dangerous waters.

A rendezvous between the French and American forces was decided upon for September 11, and Count de Fontanges raced back with this word to the French fleet. Pulaski and McIntosh left together to join their own forces at Augusta which were to spearhead the expedition. General Lincoln galloped back to his camp near Charleston to call in his scattered militia and put his troops on the march.

These American forces all reached the meeting place on the Savannah River the same day, but there was as yet no sign of the French. While waiting for them to appear, the Americans decided to send out some of Pulaski's horsemen to scout the British position on the other side of the river at Savannah. But all the ferryboats had been destroyed.

How should they cross the river? One of the soldiers found an abandoned canoe, and everyone roared with laughter when he proudly showed it to the generals. It was ridiculous to think of moving whole troops across the Savannah River in one single old battered canoe.

But Casimir had an idea. The canoe held two men. If the horses could be made to swim, in twenty or thirty trips as many volunteers and their equipment could be ferried over one by one. Thirty men could do some useful scouting about while the armies waited on the other side. General Lincoln was delighted with the idea, for as commander in chief he was anxious to know about the movements and position of the enemy.

Captain Bentalou offered to lead the expedition and everyone watched breathlessly as the first canoe pushed out into the stream, a horse swimming alongside. When it landed, thirty more men unsaddled their horses and awaited their turn. One by one they were slowly ferried to the other shore until, as the sun was setting, the twenty-fifth man reached the other side. No one had fallen in the river and the horses were safe from the alligators. Captain Bentalou sent back word that he wished to set out for Savannah without waiting for the rest of the company.

A deep swamp crisscrossed with streams surrounded Savannah on three sides. The wide Savannah River protected it on the fourth. It was a natural island fortress for the British, guarded by an impenetrable morass of quicksand and mud about three miles wide. Four wooden causeways were the only means of approach, and it was along one of these that Captain Bentalou led his horsemen in single file. The bridges over the streams had just been destroyed, and he had to chop down trees for the logs to mend them.

Had the British attacked, retreat would have been impossible. Where the causeway reached the island of Savannah, a few well-hidden English soldiers from a trench on the bluff above easily could have picked off the little band one by one as they rode into range. Bentalou saw there was a very great advantage in creeping over this last stretch under cover of darkness.

The situation of the scouting party was indeed perilous. Separated from their army by the river, their only safety was the darkness. Exhausted and fearful that their horses would stumble and be sucked deep into the bog, the men moved silently forward until they reached dry land.

The captain, after instructing his men to return and report to Pulaski if he were shot, started up the bank on foot. Hidden by the black shadow of a thick growth of scrub pine, he crept along beside the road that curved steeply up the sandy bluff on which the town of Savannah was built. There at the top, just as he had expected, were freshly dug British mounds and trenches, but they were not manned. The British forces had withdrawn inside the Savannah fortifications.

Dawn was breaking as he scrambled back down the hill. He now minutely inspected the enemy fortifications and the other three approaches to Savannah under the very noses of the British. Hazardous though it was, the scouts spent the day crouched in the bushes watching the British digging trenches. They then managed to locate the other three causeways without being seen or heard. At last, hungry and exhausted, they crawled under a bank of honeysuckle and fell fast asleep.

The following midnight, their mission completed, Bentalou was leading the weary men back to the ferry when he heard footsteps. At the challenge to halt he ordered his men to draw arms and shoot it out. Imagine his surprise to hear Pulaski call his name! Casimir and the rest of the Legion, augmented with volunteers, had all been ferried across the river in the same old canoe!

The men were so happy at meeting their friends that they almost shouted with joy. After hearing the report, Casimir ordered Bentalou to set up headquarters a few miles up the river at Cherokee Hill plantation and to rest while he gave the enemy "a little surprise."

Casimir then followed the directions Bentalou had given, led his men safely across the swamp and up the Savannah bluff. Like a bolt of lightning, he charged the northern outpost of the city, overpowered the astonished sentries, took a number of prisoners and returned to camp before Bentalou and his men had time to settle in their new quarters.

Early the next morning a stranger in a red coat was seen riding through the woods. Some of the Legion dragoons were sent after him in hot pursuit. The man was soon overtaken and brought back to headquarters. He proved to be a friendly messenger with letters to General Lincoln and Pulaski from D'Estaing informing them of the difficulty which the French were having in landing. There had been such a violent storm on the sea that for three consecutive days all the lifeboats overturned as soon as they were put in the water.

Pulaski sent the messenger, with a guide, to General Lincoln. He then gave orders to his aides to choose the men to accompany him as he was leaving at once to meet with Admiral d'Estaing. Though it was raining very heavily, and he was shaking with fever, he nevertheless jumped into his saddle and set off for the beach where the French were trying to land.

Captain Bentalou rode close beside his commander. He was fearful lest the rain-soaked branches would brush Pulaski off his horse. But by an almost superhuman effort of his will, Casimir was more alert than usual. He pointed out every broken twig or trampled blade of grass. Certain they would soon come upon a British patrol, he told his men to ride with cocked pistols.

His vigilance was soon rewarded. They had begun to cross a swamp in single file when Pulaski heard the neigh of a horse. He ordered his men back where they could hide in the tangled undergrowth while he and Captain Bentalou nonchalantly blocked the way.

A British patrol of a dozen men emerged from the swamp and were ordered to halt. Before they could draw they were surrounded, disarmed and taken prisoner. They proved to be a band of scouts, sent to report on the French landing.

Pulaski suspected that the British would send out more than one company on such an important mission. He had the men gagged, their hands tied, and their horses roped together. Appointing six guards to follow with the prisoners, he led the rest of his troop at a gallop.

On the far side of the swamp they caught sight of a man ducking behind a tree. Without a word Casimir jumped from his horse which he quickly tethered. The men, imitating every move, crept stealthily after him. As the Legion approached the thicket hiding their quarry, a soldier in British uniform started to run out. Pulaski challenged him to surrender. The man, seeing himself surrounded, raised his hands.

"I'll shoot if you make a sound," Casimir told him.

At that moment they heard a crack and roar of falling trees, and realized that the enemy must be building an outpost very close by. Casimir rushed toward the spot from which the sound had come.

There they found a startled British patrol, armed only with saws, spades and pickaxes. Pulaski shouted at them to surrender.

The British tried to escape into the forest, a few snatching up their guns as they ran. Bullets whistled through the trees, but after a brief skirmish all were surrounded and forced to give up. Now Pulaski had twice as many prisoners as men. However, rather than retrace his steps to take them back to camp, he pushed on to the coast to meet D'Estaing.

Far from letting up, the rain grew heavier with every mile. Wind carried the leaves and swaying branches like streamers before it. Great fronds of palmettos, hurled to the ground, scratched the men with their spiny stalks. The horses pranced uneasily. The men's voices could hardly be heard above the roar of the storm. But at last they reached the shore.

From the top of the dunes Pulaski looked out at the angry sea. The great French fleet lay at anchor, pitching and rolling in steep, choppy waves. It thrilled him to see the vast army spread out before him. Several thousand men were huddling about the beach fires trying to cook or dry their clothes. Others were landing in the breakers. Carrying their clothes high above their heads, they were wading ashore while sailors in water to their waists kept the rowboats from pounding on the sand. Overseeing the proceedings through his spyglass, Pulaski finally recognized the French admiral. He set off at a trot at the head of his Legion, followed by his long line of prisoners.

As Casimir rode down the dunes the French soldiers roared out in welcome. Admiral d'Estaing saw Casimir and ran to embrace him. "I knew you would be the first to come," he called to him joyfully.

D'Estaing, ruddy and tanned from his sea voyage, was energetic and swift in all his movements. As the two commanders eyed each other, an immediate friendship sprang up. D'Estaing, like Pulaski, was a leader who took the same risks as his men. His first thought had been to arrange for their shelter after the tumble most of them received in the sea.

Casimir volunteered to lead D'Estaing to his appointed headquarters, three miles south of Savannah, in Greenwich on the Wellington River. The commanders decided for the time being to take the British prisoners out to the French ships. The Englishmen were led to the shore and as they were being loaded into the rowboats, the French soldiers collected their belongings and prepared to march.

Pulaski described in detail to D'Estaing the layout of the British fortifications at Savannah and the swamp that surrounded the city. As their horses jogged through the dripping woods, he pointed out the headquarters of the American generals as well as his own. Except for the roar of wind in the trees and the spatter of driving rain it was a peaceful ride. Pulaski had indeed seen to it that the enemy feared to leave Savannah.

On the following day, without consulting the American generals, Admiral d'Estaing demanded the immediate surrender of Savannah. There General Prevost was in command. He had managed to get through from Beaufort Island, asked for time, and was granted an armistice of twenty-four hours. This concession was a fatal blunder. In his later report to Parliament, General Prevost admitted that Savannah would have fallen in ten minutes had the armistice not been granted. Since the Americans agreed, however, he was able to send for Lieutenant Maitland whom he had left in command of the eight hundred men at Beaufort and to bring up these reinforcements through secret channels to Skull Creek where they waited for the tide to come in. They eased their boats over the bar, a heavy fog helped conceal their movements and they landed in Savannah unobserved.

The British forces in Savannah had been reduced to seventeen hundred men. With the addition of Lieutenant Maitland's command, Prevost now had twenty-five hundred soldiers, not counting the blacks and Indians he had impressed into his service. He sent back word to the Americans that he intended to resist and would not surrender. That same evening, before sundown, he fired a signal for the commencement of hostilities.

Savannah at the time was a village of between three hundred and fifty and four hundred houses.

It was laid out in an oblong shape with main streets crossing at the center and smaller streets set out in rectangles. The main streets led to the causeways running north and south. On the west, the Augusta Road led across Musgrove Creek and the rice fields planted in the swamp.

Working night and day, the British strengthened their defenses. They set up fifteen batteries and built thirteen redoubts with intercommunicating lines protected by rough trenches and traps. They constructed a ditch all around the city at the edge of the swamp and destroyed all connecting causeways. They threw a boom across the harbor to protect their vessels which were lined up in battle array to rake the allied armies if they tried to reach Savannah from the northern or southern approaches along the river. In the channel they sank still more of their own ships to keep the French fleet from approaching within gunshot.

General Lincoln met D'Estaing on September 16 after the summons to surrender had been sent to the British. He was opposed to D'Estaing's plan of beginning the battle at once if the British did not surrender. He thought the British could not hold out, since the allied forces outnumbered them two to one. He said there was plenty of time. He advised dismantling the guns from the French fleet and setting them up in batteries to bombard the town. He hoped that the barrage would do so much damage that Prevost would give up without the allied soldiers having to make a charge.

From experience, Casimir knew that the siege of the town would inevitably be followed by bitter fighting, that the British would not easily give up. He did not share General Lincoln's belief that victory would be easy, that time was on their side. He urged the Americans to follow the French plan of immediate assault and when his plea failed he maintained the greatest possible vigilance. He changed headquarters every night and, as was his habit, attacked the enemy pickets in lightning raids.

Under cover of darkness his men would repair a part of the causeway, steal over and seize one of the British outposts before others could be brought to his help. Silently his lancers harried the enemy. No one knew the time or place he would strike because Casimir alone gave orders to move. His officers had such confidence in him that he never needed to hold a council where a spy might learn his next move. He always led the charge himself and took all the risks he asked of his men.

When the French batteries were finally moved into place, the bombardment of the town began. Three days of brisk fire had no effect on the British. The French naval officers began to grumble against D'Estaing. They remonstrated at his folly in keeping the fleet exposed when storms and hurricanes were blowing up the coast. Moreover, most of their guns were ashore and British ships were known to be near.

On September 22 a French attack was repulsed by the British. Next day, hidden by a thick blanket of fog, the French managed to get within three hundred yards of the enemy and to build dugouts. The British attacked the new French positions and were repulsed. On the twenty-fifth the French again opened up with a heavy bombardment and repulsed several more British sorties.

On October 2 D'Estaing ordered his naval forces to shell the town from the frigate *La Truite*, while the shore batteries smashed away. Numbers of the citizens of Savannah were killed and their houses burned, but the British installations were unharmed. This was repeated five days later with the same effect.

By now D'Estaing had become uneasy. His engineers reported that it would take ten days to build a sufficient number of new causeways across the swamp to bring in the troops necessary to force the British to surrender. Every day more of his men were being felled by dysentery because of spoiled and inadequate rations. His naval officers begged him to leave because of the tempestuous weather and its danger to the fleet. D'Estaing called a council of war.

General Lincoln and General McIntosh agreed to make an all-out attack on the British forces. Two columns of French infantry and one of American were to make a concerted attack on the same point in the right wing of the line at the same time, while pretending to assault the center and left. They thus hoped to deceive the British and force them to divide their army at three points.

Pulaski was given command of all the American and French cavalry. He was to follow the infantry as soon as a breach in the enemy's lines had been made. As an intrepid leader, skilled in hand-to-hand fighting, he was given the perilous task of being the first to enter Prevost's garrison.

Colonel Laurens, commanding the Charleston Grenadiers, was to follow him closely, behind him was to come General McIntosh leading two companies of militia. Both the French and the Americans' reserves were expected to do the mopping up under General Lincoln, who was to accept the British commander's surrender.

After the council made these plans, the allied commanders returned to their headquarters and explained them to the officers under their command. The all-out battle was set to take place early the next morning, on October 9. Every man was to be at his post by 4 a.m.

But during the night Sergeant Major James Curry of the Charleston Grenadiers, one of Colonel Laurens' men, deserted to the British and gave them complete details of the whole allied plan of attack. In the confusion of moving troops, Sergeant Curry was not missed until roll call. By then it was too late; the battle was under way.

Admiral d'Estaing personally led the French troops. He paid no attention to the advice of his engineers, and in order to avoid a long way round to reach his meeting place with Generals Pulaski and McIntosh, he plunged straight into the swamp. Naturally he had no experience with the treacherousness of such a deep, impenetrable morass. He had seen the heavy ropes of moss hanging from the trees growing out of the water and thought the men would be able to jump across the water from one tree to the next.

Had he caught the enemy unaware he might have succeeded. But the British knew from Curry that there was no real danger to their left or center. The Americans, who were making a mock attack, did not have orders to proceed when their fire was not returned. Unfortunately, they failed to draw off a single British soldier or to follow up their advantage by entering the fort from the rear.

In the meantime, the British were training all their guns on the unfortunate French caught in the swamp. Their fierce and deadly fire was creating horrible havoc. D'Estaing had plunged ahead so fast that most of his supporting troops could not keep up with him. Those who had, either drowned in the swamp or were raked by enemy guns.

Yet the French persisted, though by now things were so hopeless that the general plan of battle could not be followed. General McIntosh offered to help, but he was told to go around the swamp and lead an attack on the north, since it was obvious the French were trapped. But to do so he had to pass through the enemy line of fire and so lost many men.

Pulaski and Laurens had marched south as directed. D'Estaing and the French forces had not reached the point from which they had agreed to cross the rice fields, but Casimir heard the terrible cannonade and hurried farther south. As he came to the edge of the swamp and saw the carnage, he told the cavalry to keep back out of the line of fire while he went forward by himself. Calling Captain Bentalou to follow, he made for a little higher point of land where he could view the whole scene.

Casimir could see that the French forces had collapsed into a rout of panic-stricken men. The noise of screaming, of crashing trees, of the roar and whine of bullets was terrible. Muddy blood-soaked soldiers were scrambling over each other to escape. He saw D'Estaing fall, apparently mortally wounded. Realizing what a terrible effect this disaster would produce on the spirit of the French forces, and hoping his presence would give them fresh courage, Pulaski, without a thought for his own safety, rushed to the side of the French commander.

Rallying the men nearest him, he ordered others to carry D'Estaing away to a safer spot. By the time several more of his officers had reached the murderous spot, a piece of grapeshot, in size of a twenty-five-cent piece, struck Pulaski in the right groin. As he turned to help his beloved commander, Captain Bentalou was wounded in the back of the neck.

Before Pulaski lost consciousness he told the French officers: "Follow Captain Horry and my lancers to whom I have given orders of attack." The

French officers rallied their troops and followed the Legion which managed to assault the British parapets twice after its leader had fallen. In all the battle had lasted but fifty-five minutes when a truce was called to bury the dead. When it was seen that of the total French forces of forty-four hundred and fifty-six men, over a thousand had been killed, the Allies retired. The British had lost only one hundred and sixty-three of their army of twenty-five hundred.

The Allies were defeated. The French troops and artillery were ordered back to their ships. The Americans called off their men and abandoned Savannah.

13

A Hero's End

DUE TO PULASKI'S QUICK ACTION, D'Estaing's life had been saved. Generals Lincoln and McIntosh came to the French admiral's tent where he was being treated by his own surgeons. They praised him for his fearless action in leading his men and expressed their sorrow at the terrible losses he had sustained.

Though he was suffering severe pain, D'Estaing managed to reply. With true French gallantry he did not blame the Americans for the treachery of Sergeant Major Curry but expressed his pleasure in cooperating with the American Army. The officers parted good friends, neither blaming the other for the disastrous results of the Battle of Savannah.

The wounded Pulaski and Bentalou had been carried from the field and were also being treated in a tent by the personal surgeon of D'Estaing in consultation with the best doctors of the French fleet. But the doctors agreed that Pulaski should be moved aboard a ship where it was cooler, and away from the swarms of flies and mosquitoes buzzing about his head. They needed to operate at once and remove the grapeshot from his groin. Cannon bullets had torn another ugly wound in his body.

The American brig *Wasp* was put at the disposal of Pulaski. D'Estaing ordered his most skillful doctor to accompany Casimir as he was lowered on a stretcher into the dingy and rowed out to the ship. Mercifully he fainted with the pain and lost consciousness again.

When he next opened his eyes, he was lying in his bunk. The white curtains hung around it were moving in the gentle air blowing through the porthole. Captain Bentalou, his head swathed in bandages, was leaning over him, a glass of brandy in his hand.

"Drink this," he urged; "it will give you strength."

"Have they removed the bullets?" Casimir asked.

"Not all," Bentalou replied. "They want to try again, when you are feeling better. Drink this, while

I call the cook who has been preparing you some broth."

"Don't go. You are badly wounded yourself. I should be caring for you," Pulaski said, trying to smile.

"My wounds are just little scratches," Bentalou insisted. He hurried away to call the steward, and when he returned Pulaski was delirious. The brandy glass had spilled over the deck. He was tossing in his bunk, mumbling in Polish words Bentalou could not understand. His teeth began to chatter and his fever to mount. Greatly alarmed, Bentalou sent for the doctor.

Before the doctor returned Casimir opened his eyes, called *"Tatus*—father!" and sat up, staring wildly. The sight of Bentalou seemed to calm him. "I thought I was home," he explained. Casimir fell back exhausted and seemed to be asleep when the doctor climbed back aboard the ship.

One glance showed him how much the condition of his patient had deteriorated. The wound had ceased bleeding in an ominous fashion and red streaks of infection had begun to appear. He sent for his colleagues, who decided at once upon a second operation. But the grapeshot had mangled Pulaski too severely for them to remedy the situation.

From then on Pulaski's condition became worse. Bentalou never left his beloved commander's side. Most of the time Casimir was delirious, but occasionally his mind would clear. He would ask, "Why are we delaying, why don't we start?" Sometimes he described Winiary and his childhood, humming tunes his mother used to sing in the evenings. He would talk about old Michael, the coachman, and the cook.

His sister Anna was often in his mind. "When I am established in Charleston," he once said, "she will be so happy to think of it. She has always begged me to settle down. When the war is over I will indeed—indeed—when the British are beaten, when America is free. Now we must go on fighting until America is free."

For two days Bentalou watched his dying commander stifle his groans and, when his mind cleared, make plans for the future. Then on the third day Casimir came out of his delirium entirely. By now the gangrene had reached every part of his body, and the pain of the infection was so intense that Bentalou wondered how it was possible to endure such suffering.

But the habit of a lifetime sustained Pulaski. Now that he realized he was dying, he apologized for causing so much trouble, and begged Bentalou to rest. Though his lips were parched and cracked from fever, he still managed a smile.

When Bentalou tried to make him more comfortable, he remarked, "God is good. He lets me think clearly and pray. I have so much for which to pray; that my country will once again be free as this country surely will. All my life I have fought for freedom."

Finally a smile became fixed upon his lips. For a number of hours his fingers slipped back and forth over the medal of our Lady of Częstochowa which he always wore pinned to his breast. Then crying out "Jesus, Mary, Joseph," he died. It was October 11, 1779. Pulaski was thirty-two years old.

His body was so consumed with gangrene that it was impossible to sail his remains up the coast to Charleston for burial. Poor Captain Bentalou had to make the terrible decision to commit "to a watery grave," as he expressed it, "all that was left on earth of my beloved commander." The French fleet had stood by for three days while their most skillful surgeons had worked to save Pulaski's life. When it became clear that there was nothing more to be done, orders had been given to set sail. As they watched the body of Pulaski being slipped over the side of the *Wasp*, all their guns fired a final salute. It was their last tribute to that most noble and generous soldier who had given his life for the freedom of America in which he so confidently believed.

The brig *Wasp* entered Charleston Harbor with her flag at half mast. As she sailed through the fleet of anchored vessels, this mournful sign was repeated on them all. When they reached port, the batteries on the fort pounded out in a last salute. The news shot through the city, and the whole populace streamed to the dock.

The governor and Council of South Carolina proclaimed a day "of universal mourning," to pay homage to the gallant Pole. They decreed the "most respectful, splendid funeral honors should be paid in his memory." The quartermaster general was directed to pay for all the preparations necessary for the "melancholy solemnity."

A magnificent funeral procession was organized. Three high-ranking American and three French officers were to carry the handsome pall. The beautiful horse on which Pulaski had received his death wound was to be saddled and bridled and draped with the uniform in which he was struck down. Carrying the sword, lance and spurs, it was to follow the empty coffin. When the procession formed, such an immense crowd tried to walk in it that the line encircled the whole city of Charleston.

The procession led to the church where the army chaplain made an address. In another oration Colonel Lee of Virginia said, "Those who knew Pulaski intimately know the sublimity of his many virtues and the loyalty of his friendship." As the speeches were delivered there were tears in the eyes of the listeners. The people of Charleston had never been more united than in the sorrow they felt over the loss of so good and brave a friend.

General Lincoln wrote to tell Congress of "the loss of the late intrepid Count Pulaski," and Congress in a fine gesture commanded a splendid monument in his honor to be erected in Savannah. Instantly all the petty difficulties of supplying the Legion were forgotten as, to a man, the congressmen vied with each other in pouring out praise.

When the news reached Europe, not only his friends but his enemies mourned him. Even King Stanislaus remarked: "He died as he lived, a hero, but an enemy of kings."

Though the Battle of Savannah seemed at the time a disaster, actually it was the turning point in the war. The losses of the British during the previous summer in the retreat of Prevost to Beaufort and the constant harassment by the Legion of the remaining forces in Savannah were really very great.

The lessons taught by Pulaski finally bore fruit. Once a war is begun, to win you must seize the offensive. Even after his death, Casimir Pulaski aided the American cause for which he had given the last drop of his blood.

About the Author

Dorothy Adams was descended from the colonial Adamses, a family whose members made noteworthy contributions to the founding of the United States of America. Growing up in Boston, she attended Goucher College and for a short time was associated with the League of Nations. In 1926, while a student at the London School of Economics, she met and married Jan Kostanecki, a Polish economist and diplomat. Together, they returned to his recently restored nation of Poland. A son was born, and she gave herself to learning the language, customs and history of her new home. Dorothy came to identify personally with the patriotism of her husband's family and friends and with their enthusiasm for the work of rebuilding their nation; she was also able to assist her husband in his international diplomatic missions for the Polish government.

After her husband's tragic death in 1937 in an airplane accident, Dorothy stayed on in Poland until 1939. At that time, her American relatives, fearing the approach of war in Poland, convinced Dorothy to return to the United States. As the storm of World War II swept across her adopted country, she wrote a book called *We Stood Alone*, which recounted in personal detail the experience she knew of that stirring, pre-war era in Poland.

In this young people's biography about Casimir Pulaski, Dorothy Adams brings to life the story of someone with unquenched ideals, who, like herself, bridged the double patriotisms of Poland and America.[1]

---

[1] Information from original book jacket and a book review in *The Saturday Evening Post*, September 30, 1944.

Historical Insights

by Daria Sockey

Cavalry Hero: Casimir Pulaski
(by Dorothy Adams)

In *So Young a Queen,* the first book of the "Polish Advocates of Hope and Nationhood" Portraits, the story ended on a high note—the selfless sacrifice and wisdom of Queen Jadwiga resulted in a strong, prosperous, and Catholic Poland. A nation that became a center of trade, culture, education, and also a haven of tolerance for religious minorities.

But as *Calvary Hero* opens, nearly four centuries have passed, and Poland is dying. Surrounded by several powerful, grasping kingdoms, Poland always struggled for its existence. But a series of horrific wars in the mid-17th century, known collectively as *The Deluge*, had reduced Poland's population by 1/3 and robbed much of its treasure. By the early 18th century the weakened nation was already a protectorate of Russia: independent in theory but vulnerable to Russian political intrigue and torn by many factions. Its borders to the west and the south were being nibbled away by Prussia and Austria. Shortly after the events narrated in *Calvary Hero*, Poland disappeared from the map as an independent nation—swallowed up by Russia, Austria, and Germany (Prussia). Its resurrection wouldn't occur until 1918. (You can read about that in the next book in this series, *The Lion of Poland: The Story of Paderewski*.)

Joseph Pulaski and his sons were fighting in a hopeless cause. Their goal—Poland's freedom from Russian control—was something most Poles wanted. But too few were willing to risk everything—their property, possessions, treasure, and lives. Idealists such as the Pulaskis, with their wholehearted devotion to justice and freedom, nourished by their Catholic faith, were a vanishing species. As a result of his convictions, Casimir Pulaski lost his home and most of his family. He found himself a defeated and penniless exile with the tide of popular opinion turned against him.

Perhaps his greatest pain was to be unable to use his God-given talent as a warrior in a righteous cause. It is no wonder, then, that Casimir Pulaski chose to go to America and fight for freedom rather than to return to his beloved homeland under a pardon that stipulated a life of retirement. In the American Revolution he found a cause similar, but more hopeful than the doomed struggle to save Poland.

It is true that he experienced here some of the same problems he had in Poland: lack of appreciation from political leaders and the failure of military superiors to make optimal use of his cavalry. (It seems that God wanted Pulaski to learn the virtue of patience—a long-term project!) Despite this, America offered Pulaski more scope for his abilities than did Poland. His talent at small, "guerilla"-style actions which had been stifled in Poland came fully into play here. His talent for horsemanship and knowledge of cavalry tactics added a new weapon to the continental arsenal. Although his abilities were not thoroughly appreciated during his lifetime (except perhaps by George Washington), the cavalry training manual he wrote was used for years to come and earned him the title "Father of the US Cavalry." And probably nothing else redounds to Pulaski's glory as much as his very first adventure at the Battle of Brandywine, and might be the reason that Providence had sent him here: he saved the life of George Washington. For all we know, that rescue saved the entire American Revolution.

Pulaski did not live to see America win independence. The battle in which he died was a defeat for the American cause. But to die a hero's death on the battlefield would have been, despite the pain, a great joy for him. America's gratitude to Casimir Pulaski is evident in the many towns, bridges, parks, and naval warships that bear his name.

Set 2: Polish Advocates of

The timeline below highlights key historical events in Pulaski and

Jadwiga
1374-1399

800

Poland emerges as independent kingdom

1347
Statutes of Kazimir the Great issued in Poland

1095-1291
Series of intermittent Crusades in Europe

1384
Jadwiga crowned queen of Poland

1386
Jadwiga marries Jagiello of Lithuania, forming the Christian Polish-Lithuanian Commonwealth

1399
University of Krakow, begun by Kazimir the Great, completed

1410
Jagiello defeats Teutonic Knights at Battle of Grünwald

1573

1573
Poland becomes regular republic, with kings elected

1619-1772
Series of disastrous wars for Poland with Cossacks, Russians, and Swedes

1767
Joseph Pułaski forms Knights of the Holy Cross in Poland

1768-1772
Wars of the Bar Confederation fight for Polish-Lithuanian Commonwealth integrity

Hope and Nationhood
and around the lifetimes of Jadwiga, Casimir Ignace Paderewski

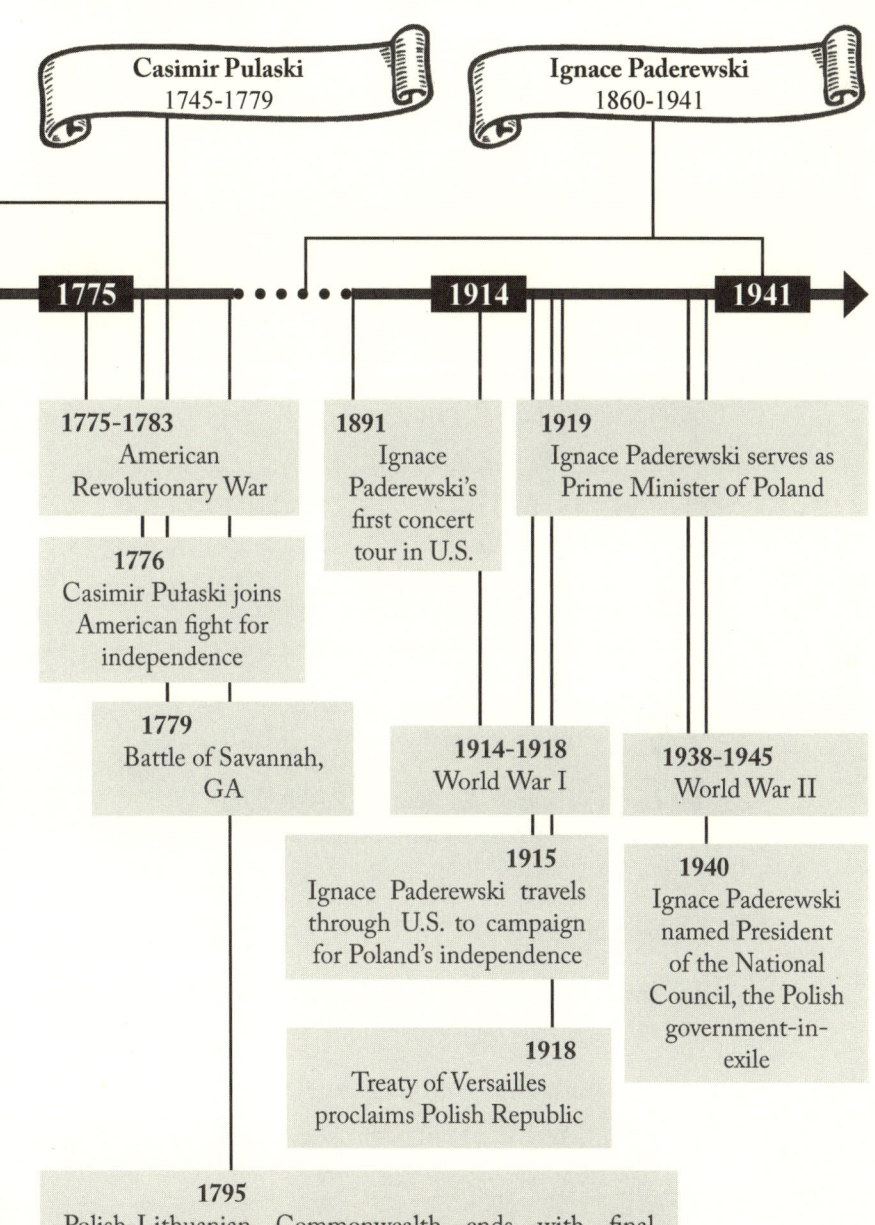

List of Titles in Portraits in Faith and Freedom

SET 1: FOUNDING VOICES FOR FREEDOM IN THE U.S.

Charles Carroll and the American Revolution
by Milton Lomask

Priest, Patriot and Leader: The Story of Archbishop Carroll
by Eva K. Betz

Mathew Carey: Pamphleteer for Freedom
by Jane F. Hindman

SET 2: POLISH ADVOCATES OF HOPE AND NATIONHOOD

So Young a Queen: Jadwiga of Poland
by Lois Mills

Cavalry Hero: Casimir Pulaski
by Dorothy Adams

The Lion of Poland: The Story of Paderewski
by Ruth and Paul Hume

SET 3: SPANISH AND MEXICAN HEROES

The Sea Tiger: The Story of Pedro Menéndez
by Frank Kolars

Padre Pro: Mexican Hero
by Fanchón Royer

SET 4: WOMEN OF FAITH AND COURAGE

Star of the Mohawk: Kateri Tekakwitha
by Francis MacDonald

Margaret Haughery: Bread Woman of New Orleans
by Flora Strousse

The Door of Hope: The Story of Katharine Drexel
by Katherine Burton

SET 5: MISSIONARIES ON THE FRONTIER

Joseph the Huron
by Antoinette Bosco

Simon Bruté and the Western Adventure
by Elizabeth Bartelme

Frontier Priest and Congressman: Father Gabriel Richard, S.S.
by Brother Alois

Black Robe Peacemaker: Pierre De Smet
by J. G. E. Hopkins

SET 6: NEW YORK AMBASSADORS OF BROTHERHOOD

Pierre Toussaint: Pioneer in Brotherhood
by Arthur and Elizabeth Sheehan

John Hughes: Eagle of the Church
by Doran Hurley

Alfred E. Smith: Sidewalk Statesman
by William G. Schofield